CHILDREN AND LEARNING
Some aspects and issues

Walter McVitty
Editor

CHILDREN
AND
LEARNING

Some aspects and issues

PRIMARY ENGLISH TEACHING ASSOCIATION

Acknowledgements:

The Editor and PETA wish to thank (a) Wadsworth Publishers for permission to reproduce the drawing on page 24, from *Psychology of Teaching*, by Guy Lefrancois, (b) The Bodley Head for permission to reproduce the picture on page 40 from *Where the Wild Things Are* by Maurice Sendak, and (c) Paramount Television for permission to reproduce the photograph on page 118.

Special thanks are due also to Brian McKeown and Karonga House Public School for the use of photographs reproduced on pages 30, 37, 45, 49, 101 and 107, and for the staff and students at Loreto Convent Junior School, Kirribilli, for being willing photographic subjects for the Editor.

ISBN 0 909955 53 0
First published October 1984
Reprinted 1985
Copyright © Primary English Teaching Association, 1984
P.O. Box 167, Rozelle NSW 2039
Printed in Australia by
Bridge Printery Pty Ltd, 29-35 Dunning Ave, Rosebery, NSW 2018

PREFACE

PETA publications have been enthusiastically received and appreciated by a countless number of classroom teachers throughout Australia—and, increasingly, by teachers overseas as well. Our publications are so highly valued by teachers because of their essentially *practical* nature. While soundly based on theory, they have always presented the best of up-to-date ideas in no-nonsense, down-to-earth, useful, workable ways.

As well as publishing much-needed "how-to" or "tips-for-teachers" publications, PETA also has an important role to play in contributing to the quality of educational thought. It is interested not only in WHAT goes on in classrooms, and HOW things are done, but also in the WHY of these things. Consequently PETA aims to add balance to its publishing program by providing stimulating and sometimes challenging discussions on a wide range of educational ideas and issues—hence *Children and Learning*, PETA's second *Issues* book.

This new book brings together fourteen thought-provoking articles about aspects of children and learning, under three headings. Part One offers us the opportunity to think about our own philosophies of education and challenges us to clarify our ideas and perhaps modify our approaches to children and teaching. As well as containing statements of personal philosophies, it also includes Brian Jacka's brilliantly clear and compressed survey of the whole range of beliefs underlying major educational practices. It has been said that a year's membership of PETA is the equivalent of a major in-service course—the same might be said of this article alone!

Part Two looks at issues in literacy learning and includes what might at first *appear* to be a "revisionist" approach to "process-conference" writing. It argues that only a very small percentage of children's writing, overall, ever needs revising; that correct spelling, handwriting and grammar *are* important, and that conferences can actually be a waste of time. Its author is none other than Donald Graves! However, as always, what he has to say makes plain good sense. In similar vein, Bob Walshe extends our understanding of writing by suggesting that the thought processes and methods employed in writing are the same as in other "disciplines"—as in, say, *scientific* inquiry.

Part Three examines issues in learning through a wide range of communication and information media.

There is insufficient space here to list every item—each is interesting and worthwhile.

PETA is interested in shifting the focus from *teaching* to *learning*—from teaching *what* to think to learning *how* to think. This ideal applies to teachers as well as children. It is hoped that *Children and Learning* will provide teachers—and parents too—with a wealth of stimulating thought within the range of issues chosen for this particular publication, and that it will lead to productive discussion. Such thought and discussion offer teachers opportunities for change and growth—which is what we always hope to do for the children we teach.

Walter McVitty
Editor

CONTENTS

Changing views
about learning

SOME HALF-TRUTHS ABOUT LEARNING

Barry Dwyer
President, P.E.T.A.
Director (Eastern Region), Catholic Education Office, Sydney.

Learning is at the very heart of our profession. After all, the main purpose of schooling is to help this process to happen; our life's commitment as teachers is to assist children *to learn how to learn*.

Yet how often do we really take time out to consider the critical question of how learning actually occurs? Myths about it abound and, in just about every one of them, there is some element of truth that bestows undeserved respectability.

In this article I want to reflect briefly on some of the most common half-truths about learning.

1. **Learning is the act of acquiring and retaining information.**

The corollary of this half-truth is that teaching is the act of transmitting facts and of helping learners to store them in some cerebral warehouse.

Now this view has considerable acceptance in the world at large which sees the quiz champion—with "a mind like an encyclopaedia"—as being the master of the art, the learner of learners.

Good teachers must be good fact-dispensers. "Do you think you'll be able to put it across?" is the question often asked of would-be teachers by relatives and friends whose theory of pedagogy is built on the image of a full jug pouring the good oil into rows of empty vessels.

From this perspective, the job of students is to "pay attention" and remember what they are told by teachers who are purveyors of information and whose tools of trade are textbooks, tabulations and tests.

Of course, there is something in this half-truth. Good learners are certainly skilled data-collectors. They acquire many facts and are able to draw from this store to solve problems, explain aspects of their world and meet immediate needs.

On the other hand, they are not mere walking data-banks. Their real skill lies in seeing relationships amongst pieces of information, in composing meaning, making sense and struggling towards better understanding. Not only do they gather and use facts efficiently but they make judgements about them and develop essential concepts. These processes are at the centre of the type of learning that makes us truly human.

2. Learning is a somewhat unnatural activity.

Because it is not natural, children generally don't like doing it. So teachers have to turn themselves inside out trying to motivate the unwilling to do the intrinsically uninteresting.

True or false? Well, it's certainly true that constructive learning can be hard work. This is particularly the case if we seek to promote it in dull and lifeless contexts, if the learner doesn't see the sense of it, or if the physical and psychological constraints are such that the learner has no real stake in the proceedings, no "ownership" of the task, and no room to move. Then, most certainly, learning will be difficult and the result often disappointing.

In such cases, the teacher must resort to extrinsic motivation, to external rewards and tokens (stars, stamps and the like) to encourage apathetic youngsters to exert themselves and get off their collective posterior.

On the other hand, *learning is what children do best.* Synonymous with growth, it is the most *natural* of all human activities.

In fact, children never stop learning. In classrooms where this truth is recognised, an observer is most likely to witness purposeful activities, various forms of experimentation with language and objects, an encouragement of risk-taking, and a tolerance of error and approximation by means of which natural learners work their way to meaning and accuracy.

3. Learning is best undertaken in a structured, orderly manner.

Break down learning into logical steps, people advise. Specify your objectives; express them in terms of behaviours that can be measured; separate the sub-skills; keep to the script; ready now, 1 . . . 2 . . . 3 . . .!

This is a very attractive proposition. In a no-nonsense world it sounds like good common sense. And, certainly, there's some truth in it. A good teacher knows about working towards attainable goals, and about sequencing and pacing. There's something in a predictable learning environment, too, that provides the psychological safety within which constructive learning can flourish.

However, the more precise and clinical we become, the less room there is for genuine exploration of ideas, for reflection, for discovering, for the "Eureka!" experience.

The "disorder" that is often allowed to develop in the orderly classroom is sometimes very appropriate for the best learning.

Frank Smith, denying that writing is a linear, left-to-right process, puts it this way:

> Writing can be done in several places and directions concurrently, and is as easily manipulated in space as it is in time. Texts can be constructed from writing done on separate pieces of paper, in note-books, on index cards, or on chalk boards at the same time that a main draft is being produced. Words and lines can be moved around on a page just as pages themselves can be reshuffled into different sequences. Writing is a plastic art. (*Language Arts*, Vol. 58, No. 7, Oct. 1981.)

All kinds of good learning may require an initial buzzing con-fusion, the opportunity to shuffle and search, to read and reflect, to argue, to express doubts . . . to scrap the whole thing and start again.

When we really think about it, we must admit that our most important learning—how to talk, interact, relate and so on—is not done in any systematic way. It is mastered so often casually, informally, incidentally, even accidentally.

4. Learning is tied to instruction.

It is certainly true that instructors can help learners to learn. It is quite false, however, to view the learner as the passive partner in the process.

In reality, learning is a most personal activity. This is particularly so in the mastery of literacy, where teachers have become increasingly aware of the limitations of instruction. Children learn to read and write by reading and writing. Caring adults provide a context and an encouragement but, the more they stress teacher-instruction over pupil-activity, the less effective learning will be.

This fact requires frequent repetition as computers and other items of technology begin to find their ways into our classrooms. It would be a tragedy of major proportions if we were to accept anything smacking of mass standardisation of content and process in education. Instructional programs that do not encourage inquiry and creative thinking, and that hamper the development of personal learning styles and ways of making sense of experience, have a very limited place amongst our resources.

5. Learning is the same for everyone.

A strong case exists for claiming that, in a democratic society, there is a common body of knowledge, skills, attitudes and values that all pupils should have the opportunity to master or acquire.

It is another thing altogether to suggest that all learners should learn the same things in the same way and complete appropriate tasks at approximately the same time.

Deeply embedded in our professional wisdom is the knowledge that individuals differ greatly in their levels and rates of development and in their learning styles. Any suggestion that there is one single approach to learning collides head-on with reality and, if acted upon, is likely to stifle the child's natural curiosity and competence in personal learning.

6. Teachers are the experts.

Certainly, good teachers are important models. They also provide resources and create environments that stimulate curiosity and provoke thinking. They are accurate observers who offer personal encouragement and help their students to become better learners.

But the best teachers are those who show their pupils how to take control of their own learning. They see their role as empowering or liberating their young charges, assisting them to become self-directed, to find their own meaning and to develop their own ways of mastering their environment.

Despite all the theories and observations at our disposal, the knowledge we have of human learning is surprisingly small.

We do know that both imitation and trial-and-error are vitally important in elementary learning. We also know that what the learner brings to a task—including a view of self—is critical in determining what and how learning will take place.

We are acutely aware of the importance of play, of inter-action, of hands-on activity and of maturation in determining learning outcomes. And we know the importance of teachers who create a stimulating environment, who organise and struc-ture activities and develop resources, who help children identify and work towards attainable goals and who demon-strate the types of behaviour that allow complex human learn-ing to occur.

While our ignorance is considerable, we have available to us some basic truths that we can confidently turn to in looking for ways to help children become better learners and more effec-tive human beings.

Helping children become better learners.

LEARNING IN SCHOOL— WHAT AND HOW?

John Vaughan
Former Assistant Director-General
N.S.W. Department of Education

1. TEACHER, PUPIL, PARENT

For each of some 200 days of the school year children spend about six hours in the care of teachers. In this 14% of total annual time, many parents, and the community at large, expect schools to work miracles of teaching-learning. These expectations are not always realistic; indeed they are not always desirable in terms of child development. Too frequently they are based upon outmoded notions of the nature and purposes of education, derived from experiences of today's adults in schools of thirty, forty, fifty years ago, when the world was a different place.

What is happening in schools? What effects do schools have on pupils? The pedant might ask: "What is the effect on individual behaviour and on group dynamics of the formal educational process?" The parent of the individual child is more likely to ask, reasonably, simply and pertinently: "What did you learn at school?"

Tom Paxton presents some delightfully satirical answers to this question in the American context (vide *Teaching as a Subversive Activity*, Postman and Weingartner, New York, Delacorte Press, 1970). Similar answers are derivable from the conventional wisdom, the folk lore, the shibboleths of any society. Paxton emphasises historical and social "facts" which the community regards as being beyond the need for verification. And in most communities the child's answer will probably include some number of "facts" of no immediate application and the spelling of certain words, not part of that child's written vocabulary.

To the extent that these are, indeed, the things which the child learns, they derive from the notion that the all-wise

7

teacher knows what should be learnt—and the child falls into line. The teacher who is successful in passing on the conventional wisdom in this way is most likely to meet with community approval.

2. MIND-STOCKING THEORY

Despite the fact that it has so frequently and effectively been discredited, the mind-stocking theory of education lives on. One has only to read the daily press or partake of radio or television programs to discover that there are those who fervently believe that there is a body of knowledge, a package of verities, a collection of precepts which teachers should use to stock the minds of children and thus equip them for life in the world of today and tomorrow. It is necessary only to appreciate the exponential increase in the body of knowledge, the falsity of many of the verities, the irrelevance of certain of the precepts, to recognise the futility of such a belief.

3. INQUIRY

Education must increasingly be concerned with experiencing, investigating, communicating, with inquiring and discovering. Learning is not achieved by a teacher declaiming to a learner. *Active involvement* of the learner is essential. Learning occurs when, facing a discerned problem, the learner inquires, hypothesises, tests. Learning involves application of facts, principles and theories in new situations, and assimilation of new facts and ideas. It has to do with making judgements based on clear criteria. Learning is not a matter of passive acceptance but of active critical thinking.

This is no new idea. Herbert Spencer held that "children should be led to make their own investigations and draw their own inferences. They should be told as little as possible and induced to discover as much as possible". Socrates promoted the cause of inquiry. But to refer to the "Spencer technique" or the "Socratic method" is to succumb to the naming syndrome, rather than to promote the cause of learning. Action is what counts.

Inquiry, of course, is not always appreciated, the critical mind not always applauded. They bring discomfort to the comfortable. It is much easier to assume that the status quo is ultimate and beyond inquiry, that knowledge and culture exist in a state of perfection, awaiting transmission.

Scribes, however, are no longer recording wisdom. Ours is a world of television and computer. Our mental horizon is not where sky and sea meet: it is out among the planets.

Educationally, the Active Intellect Hypothesis has supplanted the Absorption Hypothesis. It is no longer sensible merely to cover the course because, to the extent that we presume to know what the course is, it is either inadequate or irrelevant, or both.

4. PRODUCT AND PROCESS

Teachers are in the business of promoting understanding through inquiry and the application of scientific method. Where once concentration was on *product* (the fund of knowledge acquired) it must now be on *process* (the acquisition, organisation, retention and application of information). Most useful for learners is knowledge involving concepts which can be used repeatedly in simplification, in acquisition of further knowledge, in the integration of the old with the new.

5. DISCOVERY IN CONTEXT

Discovery learning is the basis of understanding. Problems are discerned and pursued in an environment. Traditional problems of isolationism and the "tyranny of distance" have vanished. Young people today are living through problems of urban aggregation, environmental pollution, disposal of the wastes of affluence, sexual permissiveness, drug availability, primaeval violence bursting through social veneer, national and international misunderstanding, atomic fission and fusion. They are, because they must be, seekers of truth, pursuers of purpose, searchers after aims for personal and social living in a world of conflicting values, not clarified by adult double-think and double-talk or the gobbledegook of older generations.

6. CONTENT AND METHOD

Traditionally, the educational process has been seen as a loose association between two components. The first, the important thing, is the *content*—the "stuff" to be taught. This is carefully stated in the syllabus, expanded (and frequently misrepresented) in the textbook and arranged in the program. The other component is the *method*, too frequently regarded as a secondary matter.

Above all else, the concepts of inquiry and discovery in the educational operation emphasise the fact that method is not an *incidental* in teaching-learning but is, indeed, the *core* of the operation.

Genuine learning is an active, not a passive, activity. As Rousseau exhorted, two centuries ago: "Teach by doing wherever you can, and only fall back upon words when doing is out of the question".

Too frequently has it been the case that what children *do* in the classroom is accept what the teacher has to *say*, learn the material the teacher presents, remember the content and re-present it in response to "testing".

7. THE RIGHT ANSWER

Thus we come to the teaching-learning tragedy of the "right answer". (See *Teaching as a Subversive Activity*, op. cit.) When it is assumed that the material presented in the classroom is definitive and unchallengeable, that the teacher knows the answers and that the most effective measure of pupil performance is assessment of the facility with which matching answers can be dredged out from the recesses of the learner's mind, then discovery is at an end.

How much more productive may be the part answer, the incorrect answer which leads to the next question, or the question sequential to the initial question, seeking clarification. How much more educative may be a whole complex of associated questions designed to create order out of chaos, to develop from a plethora of specifics a useful generalisation.

How much more creative may be the question which raises doubts about the whole of the material presented. Is it fact, opinion or fiction? What is the source? Is that source acceptable?

The pupil who begins to ask questions like these is creating a personal structure of inquiry, is evaluating the environment, is developing independence and a capacity to make judgements. This involves self-generating intellectual activity as opposed to making responses to Pavlovian verbal stimuli.

8. EFFECTIVE LEARNING

Effective learning flows from a willingness and an ability to face problems and to seek answers, undeterred by apparent difficulties, spurred on by challenging situations. This is a process clearly visible in the learning of Galileo, of Newton, of Einstein.

Certainly it is important to give a child opportunities to succeed and to recognise his/her achievements. This does not mean, however, that education is all softness and ease; it does not mean that lavish praise is handed out for mediocre effort, for useless answers to inconsequential questions.

Success needs to be achieved in worthwhile endeavours: pupils need to learn to deal with reasonable challenge. Thus will they gain intellectually.

Effective learning involves making judgements and decisions. Frequently it involves rejection of that conventional wisdom which may be merely enshrined ignorance. Acceptors of conventional wisdom have, in their time, believed in a flat earth, the five element theory, the non-navigability of outer space and formal grammar as the basis of creative writing. It's just a question of which wisdom happens to be conventional—and where and when.

Effective learning involves willingness to re-learn, to change one's mind in the face of new evidence or more critical examination of old evidence. As J.M. Keynes once said to his denigrators: "When the facts change, I change my mind. What do you do?" Effective learning rejects the twin concepts of a mind so open as to be creative of nothing but a draught and so impervious that it fanatically denies the obvious.

Effective learning is flexible but not necessarily speedy. Too frequently jumping to conclusions leads to landing in the deep end of the pool and threshing the water in frenzied attempts to stay afloat. Effective learning involves recognition and examination of relevant data, logical hypothesising and testing.

Effective learning distinguishes clearly between fact and opinion, between proven conclusion and tentative assumption. (See *Aims of Secondary Education in N.S.W.*—N.S.W. Department of Education, 1973.)

Effective learning demands of the learner a realistic evaluation of personal capacities, progress and decisions, in order to avoid that fanaticism which involves redoubling of efforts when goals are no longer perceived.

How may the teacher best promote the cause of effective learning? Perhaps most important is the development of an attitude which rejects a definitive view of material to be learnt, so that teaching has nothing to do with absorption and regurgitation of ex-cathedra statements.

Success needs to be achieved in worthwhile endeavours.

11

The teacher concerned about effective learning brings the pupil into contact with thought-provoking discovery-prompting situations. Such a teacher recognises that learning frequently departs from ordered sequences, makes insightful leaps and incorporates elements of serendipity. Such a teacher is aware that, in the field of learning, to pursue is often better than to arrive—that in the development of the human mind there is no terminus.

An educated person is not one with a pressure-pak head which will give forth soporific vapour at the push of a button but rather is one endlessly engaged in processes of observing and classifying, questioning and defining, conceptualising and generalising. An educated person, always aware of the realities of personal limitations and the limitations of others, has a passionate concern for pushing back the frontiers of ignorance.

9. REALITY PRINCIPLE

There are people on a well-balanced diet who insist on popping vast quantities of vitamin pills on the assumption that they "must be good for you". There are those who, with equal lack of justification, are prepared to administer shots of grammar, arithmetic or spelling with complete disregard for the educational needs of the individual child. It is possible for the school to inflict on pupils "things which are good for them" or things simply presumed to be intrinsically "good". There is little purpose in such an activity.

The situation is more serious when such material squeezes out from the curriculum things of value. For example, the child being subjected to a well-intentioned lesson on the use of the question-mark may well be failing to ask any questions at all when confronted with a television advertisement which claims that a certain brand of paste will repair holes in teeth. Many purposeful and useful lessons in communication can arise from a practical examination of the deliberately misleading and false use of language in advertising.

Organisational requirements sometimes countermand sensible educational activity. I recently encountered a lad denied classroom progression to a cursive style of handwriting (a skill, incidentally, in which he is quite proficient) because two members of the class "are not yet ready"!

The teaching of things which are beyond the bounds of the reality principle tends to be the beginning of a sequence of meaningless activities. Useless content is followed by stereotyped questions to elicit answers which satisfy the needs of the game but do little or nothing to promote understanding. In a lesson, allegedly on the topic of "place value", a teacher wrote on the chalkboard "2,1,3" and asked: "What can you make of that?" When a child, with unchallengeable logic, replied: "6", the teacher responded: "No, no; you don't see what I mean. Don't you see that we can make, 213, 123, 321 and so on?" Doubtless the child could appreciate that, but the purpose and methodology of the lesson are open to question. Emphasis on "seeing what *I* mean" implies: "*Your* thinking must be convergent with *mine*". There will be no significant leap in learning from this launching pad. For effective learning to occur, the learner must discern personal purpose in the problem, must make personal discoveries, must make personal growth.

10. UNIT OF LEARNING

Schools commonly design teaching-learning programs in terms of "subjects" or, more pretentiously, "disciplines". This is a concession to organisational convenience rather than a contribution to learning. The hard fact is that the boundaries which encompass subjects are broad, permeable bands of grey. The good teacher is not simply master of a subject and related techniques but rather takes a broad view of education, encompassing a kaleidoscopic structure of learning situations involving a complex of subjects.

The *Supplement to the Aims of Primary Education in N.S.W.* (Department of Education, 1977), presents the teaching-learning activities of Investigating, Communicating and Expressing as three interlocking circles. In the centre is the figure of a child, impinging upon each circle. And each circle encompasses a number of contributory activities. For example, Communicating includes the "subjects" of *reading, writing, spelling* and *handwriting*. To these are added other Communicating skills, such as *speaking*. What a remarkable, all-encompassing "subject" this is.

Investigating encompasses certain fundamental learning activities—inferring, predicting, questioning, approximating, calculating, measuring, comparing, hypothesising, grouping known concepts. These are not traditional "subjects" but they are fundamental to inquiry and discovery. It is interesting to note that by 1982 (*Social Studies K-6*, N.S.W. Department of Education) the three circles are presented as merging rather than interlocking and that, rather than a child in isolation, pairs and groups of children are engaged in learning activities, thus promoting the aim of the development of the individual in social context. All of this serves to emphasise *that process rather than product is at the heart of the educational activity, that the focus of the enterprise is people, not subjects.*

Teaching-learning is most productive under the guidance of an enlightened teacher who sees education as a unified process and helps pupils to integrate the contribution of "subjects" into a meaningful totality. Thus may children come to see the school and the world not as an inchoate collection of fragments but as a unified whole.

11. COMMUNICATION

Over the past quarter century schools have been rapidly technologised. Into classrooms have come teaching machines, reading rate controllers, projectors, radios, overhead projectors, tape recorders, television sets, video-recorders and computers. From the point of view of effective learning, none of these machines is either inherently good or inherently bad. It is what is done with them that counts. Learning can still occur with a teacher sitting on one end of a log and a learner on the other—if the teacher engages in the task of getting the mind of the learner to work in creative ways. Learning can fail to occur in a classroom filled with the most sophisticated gadgetry. If the gadgetry is used simply to present the material of the course—the content, the stuff to be learnt—then the potential of technological input will never be realised.

Fortunately, despite the following which it has long commanded, the Absorption approach to education never has worked. This is why those who believe in it are inevitably disappointed with the results and tend to blame the learners, frequently asserting that they won't work hard enough. The Absorption proponents fail to recognise that not all learners perceive, categorise, generalise and develop understandings in the same way. Lapps, first learning the rudiments of written language, did so, not by trying to manipulate an incomprehensible pencil, but by coiling a familiar rope upon the ground.

It is not beauty alone which is in the eye of the beholder. Every individual interprets what he or she sees in terms of previous experience, of mental set, of all those factors which constitute a personality. In short, what the learner brings to a situation conditions what is taken from it. What occurs is not an act of conservation but of transformation.

Describing a skill does not lead to its acquisition. Presenting a concept does not necessarily result in its comprehension. For the skill and the concept to be internalised, the learner must be active in inquiring, experimenting and discovering.

The moment an idea passes from one mind to another it changes. This is why so much fruitless discussion occurs in the consideration of fundamental concepts such as "democracy", "socialism", "the economy", "the national good"—and even "education". Individuals generate ideas within the confines of their own "thought cages" and toss them towards the "thought cages" of others—only to have them bounce off the wires.

Real communication involves a great deal of explanation, exploration, investigation and definition. It involves people in understanding and revealing their credos and in appreciating that the credos of others may be quite different. In fact, it involves recognition that there is no such thing as an objective person. One who begins a discussion by saying, "Looking at the question objectively . . ." is certain to present a case based on preconception and prejudice. This is not to denigrate people for their beliefs. It is simply a statement of the fact that decision-making has a values input.

Pupils, therefore, at appropriate stages of development, "should be encouraged to:
  • examine, clarify and formulate their values;
  • understand the ideas, values, feelings, goals and concerns of others;
  • see clearly the relevance of values to decision-making;
  • make inferences about the consequences of holding particular values and beliefs in different situations . . ."

(*Aims of Secondary Education in N.S.W.* op. cit.)

12. REVELATION

Let the writer of this article hurry to state that it is, indeed, a position paper. It states his position, reveals his educational values system, pleads his case. It is a personal reflection, not a learned dissertation.

The writer's hope is that the reader will be stimulated to engage in the educationally productive tasks of examining the data, analysing the arguments, identifying the facts, opinions and biases, testing the hypotheses, critically appraising, synthesising and making personal judgements. These activities are the *what* and the *how* of learning.

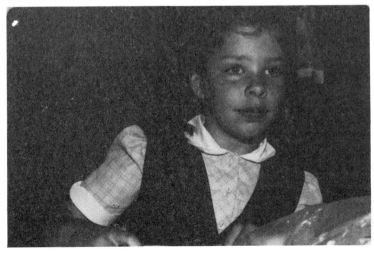

ASSUMPTIONS AND THEORY UNDERLYING EDUCATIONAL PRACTICE

Brian Jacka
Institute of Early Childhood Development,
Melbourne College of Advanced Education

The purpose of this article is to explore assumptions and theory which underly current educational practice. The study is intended to provide a guide for teachers in developing, justifying and evaluating their curricula and teaching methods. With the developing trend in Australia towards greater local control over appointment of staff and approval of curricula, teachers at all levels—early childhood, primary and secondary —are finding increasing pressure to justify their educational programs to a progressively more literate and educationally sophisticated community. The author hopes that the following will assist teachers to do this more effectively.

THE RELATION BETWEEN PRACTICE, THEORY AND PHILOSOPHY

It is useful at the outset to define a few key terms.

- *Educational practice* refers to a particular body of planned activities intended to foster the intellectual, social, emotional or motor development of the child.
- A *theory*—and, more particularly for our purposes, a psychological theory—is "a set of related principles that explain or predict the course of man's development" (Seaver and Cartwright, 1977, p. 309).
- A *philosophy* (or *ideology*, to use Kolberg and Mayer's term) is regarded as a general view or perspective on the world and on the nature of human beings and their development within it.

16

Educational practice, psychological theory and philosophy can be related in the form of a hierarchy. Consider, for example, *open education*. One popular interpretation of "openness" focuses on approaches to teaching and learning which emphasise individual discovery, personal responsibility for learning, and the quality of interpersonal relations between teacher and learner. A study of the literature (Jacka, 1974) shows that the rationale for these open practices is drawn largely from the theorising of humanistic psychologists such as Abraham Maslow and Carl Rogers. Underlying such theory is a variety of assumptions and values concerning the nature of human beings and the way they develop and learn, which, collectively, constitute a philosophy. Diagrammatically, the relation between practice, theory and philosophy can be represented as follows:

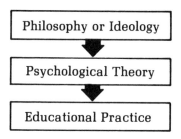

It should be recognised that *more than one theory* may derive from, or be consistent with, a particular philosophy. Similarly, a number of different educational practices may stem from one psychological theory.

Seaver and Cartwright, while recognising that many educational practices employed by teachers may not be consistent with theory, put forward a number of reasons why teachers should attempt to analyse the assumptions and theoretical rationale that underly their educational practice in order to achieve consistency. Such consistency permits a rationalisation of competing practices, since a basis is provided for their evaluation and adoption; and theory permits the reasoned development of new practices. When one looks, for example, at the plethora of approaches to the teaching of reading that have been thrust before teachers over the last couple of decades— Words in Colour, i.t.a., Breakthrough to Literacy, Distar, Phonics, S.R.A. Laboratories and so on—the force of the argument becomes apparent.

THREE PHILOSOPHICAL PERSPECTIVES

Kolberg and Mayer (1972) and Seaver and Cartwright (1977) identify three broad categories of psychological theory, each of which derives from a different philosophy or ideology concerning the source and nature of human learning and development:

- At one extreme is **romantic** or **maturational** theory which regards human development and behaviour as primarily a function of *biological* or *genetic* factors.
- At the other extreme is **behaviourist** theory which views *environmental influences* as all important.
- A third perspective, called **interactionist**, holds that, while human development is influenced by both genetic and environmental factors, the key determinant in development is the person's *autonomous self-organisation*.

Each of these perspectives is treated in some depth below.

1. THE MATURATIONAL PERSPECTIVE

Maturational philosophy assumes that innate factors are the prime determinants of development. Patterns and stages of development, psychological as well as physical, are laid down in the genes at the point of conception and unfold in a defined sequence. Kolberg and Mayer (1972) liken development of the child under this ideology to that of a plant. While the environment impinges on development, it does so "by providing the necessary nourishment for the naturally growing organism" (p. 455). The emphasis on fixed stages of growth, and genetically programmed rates of progress through the stages, has led to the maturationist ideology being labelled *predeterminist*.

Two major theories of development and learning can be considered under this ideology:

(a) the **normative** theory of Arnold Gesell and
(b) the **psychoanalytic** theory of Sigmund Freud and Eric Erikson.

Gesell is best known for the pioneering work he undertook in observing children's growth and behaviour, from which norms representing "average" or "typical" development were derived. While initial studies concentrated on physical and motor growth, his later work broadened to include behaviours influenced by psychological variables. The tables of norms derived from those studies provided guidelines for judging whether a child was "retarded", or "advanced", or "normal".

Normative Theory—implications for teachers

For the teacher, Gesell's normative theory has had at least two main legacies. The first derives from the assumption that the norms record largely the unfolding of internal, genetically programmed traits. If development is predetermined, it follows that the teacher's role should be to "bide her time until the teachable moment arrives through the methodological process of maturation" (Frost and Kissinger, 1976, p. 105). This role should involve an emphasis upon observation to assess the child's developmental needs, and the provision of a supportive educational environment that meets those needs. The approach to program planning in Australian kindergartens in the past, and to some extent today, reflects Gesell's influence. The maxim recited by many a kindergarten teacher-in-training that "learning waits on maturation" was evidence of this influence.

The second legacy relates to the use of standardised tests. The development of norms implies the use of some measuring instrument. Gesell's studies contributed to the growth in popularity of tests which identified developmental tasks and stages, and which permitted the teacher to establish the developmental level of the child. These data could then form the objectives for the planning of individual educational programs for children. Gesell's influence in this area remains significant in pre-school and junior primary programs in Australia today.

Psychoanalytic Theory

Psychoanalytic theory, developed by Sigmund Freud and extended by clinicians such as Anna Freud and Eric Erikson, leans heavily on biological factors to explain behaviour. When born, the child carries a reservoir of psychic energy called the *id* which is composed of two groups of powerful instincts: *Eros*—the life instinct, described as constructive, life seeking and self preserving, and *Thanatos*—the death instinct, which is the source of aggression, self-destruction and inhibition. The *id* energies are unconscious, irrational and seek immediate and complete gratification. They operate according to the *pleasure principle* and know no restraint. But the child lives in an environment in which unbridled instincts cannot be satisfied without restraint. Hence the development of the *ego*, which balances the demands of the *id* against the constraints of the social and physical environment. Later, with the development of the *super ego*—which comprises the conscience and ego ideal of the child—the *ego* must balance the demands of the *id* against both the constraints of the environment and the demands of the *super ego*.

The biological basis of psychoanalytic theory extends to the concept of stages. The child, in progressing towards psychosexual maturity, moves through an invariate, genetically determined sequence of stages: *oral, anal, genital* (or phallic or Oedipal) and *latency*. The manner in which the child moves through these stages, including the way in which conflicts are resolved, influences personality development at later stages. For example, during the oral phase (the first year) in which psychic energy is concentrated on the mouth, satisfaction of the child's needs is likely to develop an attitude of trust in the environment. Conversely, if this period is not a satisfying experience, an underlying feeling of mistrust of the environment may develop, and remain as a personality trait through later life.

Erikson's Developmental Stages

Eric Erikson, extending Freud's theory, has identified a sequence of eight stages of growth leading towards the mature, healthy ego (personality). A critical *task* is associated with each stage, the resolution of which influences future stages and the eventual health and strength of the ego. For the teacher working with children and adolescents, five of the eight stages are relevant:

- The critical task for the *oral* or *sensory stage* has been identified as the development of trust in the social and physical environments.
- In the *anal* or *muscular stage* (second year) successful resolution sees the beginnings of autonomy and self-control, while failure leads to underlying shame and doubt.
- Between 3 and 5 or 6 years, the child is in the *genital* or *locomotor stage*, a period during which the Oedipal (boy) and Electra (girl) crises must be resolved, leading to the formation of conscience. A negative outcome is reflected in guilt feelings that permeate the personality, while a positive resolution is reflected as initiative, enthusiasm and direction in the child's interaction with the environment.
- In the *latency* (primary school) period, success leads to attitudes of industry and competence as distinct from feelings of incompetence and inferiority if failure is experienced.
- The fifth stage—*adolescence*—sees the individual attempting to establish an identity, a process which involves defining who he or she is and what his or her role in life will be. Failure to achieve identity leads to feelings of role diffusion and insecurity.

Psychoanalytic Theory—implications for teachers

There are a number of implications for educational practice which flow from psychoanalytic theory. The aims of the pre-school or school program should reflect a concern to help the child in his or her development towards a mature personality. Erikson's stages identify a number of the qualities of this personality, e.g. trust, autonomy, initiative, competence and identity, each of which the teacher should be consciously fostering. Psychoanalytic theory places stress upon the development of *ego strength*—of a mature, realistic, autonomous self-concept. This involves the development of an understanding of oneself and of an awareness of the relationship between oneself and others. *Consistent failure in school, a rigid school environment, minimum pupil social interaction, and autocratic teaching methods are unlikely to be the most effective means of developing such self-awareness and strength of ego.*

Possibly the most well-known school operated on psychoanalytic principles is A.S. Neill's *Summerhill*, in England. Psychoanalytic theory provides, indirectly, a rationale for the nursery school movement in England, and for a number of early childhood programs in the United States, such as Bank Street in New York, which, to varying extents, draw upon Erikson's theory in emphasising healthy personality development and the conditions that promote such development. More generally, maturational theory can be seen as providing a rationale for the deschooling movement which flowered in the 1960s (Kolberg and Mayer, 1972).

2. THE BEHAVIOURIST PERSPECTIVE

In contrast to maturational ideology, behaviourism places emphasis upon the influence of *environmental factors* in development. Central to this philosophy is the assumption that "man grows to be what he is made to be by his environment" (Langer, 1969, p. 4). Behaviourism, which had its formal beginnings at the turn of this century, derived in part as an attempt by psychologists to apply the experimental techniques of the physical sciences to the study of behaviour, in the hope that the obvious gains of the physical sciences could be replicated in the behavioural sciences. The chemist and physicist focused on the objective measurement of physical stimuli, and on the reactions of the environment to these stimuli. From these observations, laws or principles relating stimuli and reactions (responses) were developed. For example, heat (a stimulus) when applied to steel produces expansion (a response), from which, over repeated trials in which the temperature is varied and all other variables controlled, a principle relating heat and expansion is derived. In the same manner, it was argued, psychologists could measure stimuli impinging on an organism, and the organism's responses to those stimuli, and thus derive laws relating these stimuli and responses (hence the term S-R psychology).

Learning, defined as *a change in response to a stimulus*, could thus be objectively studied and the "laws of learning" established. In turn, just as the physicist, through knowing laws relating to the physical environment, could "engineer" the physical environment, so the psychologist (and the teacher), by knowing the "laws of learning", could condition or "engineer" behaviour change: the teacher would thus become a *behavioural engineer*.

Conditioning

One of the first behaviourist researchers was Pavlov, who pioneered *classical conditioning* as a form of learning. In this process, a previously neutral stimulus (e.g. a bell), by being paired with another stimulus (e.g. food powder) which elicits a particular desired response (in this case, salivation), comes to elicit the same response. As the bell is now associated with a new behaviour (salivation), learning is said to have occurred. This form of conditioning has been shown to underly much learning in the *affective* area—attitudes, fears, preferences, and interests. For example, in an early (and unethical) experiment J.B. Watson conditioned 18-month-old Albert, who loved his furry white rabbit, to fear the animal by repeated pairing of a loud sound with the appearance of the animal. However, there was also some "good" news. By pairing the animal with a pleasant stimulus, Watson was able, over repeated trials, to reverse the outcome.

The process of classical conditioning (even if unintended) can be seen at work in the school. For example, the misbehaving child may be given "lines", an essay, or some other written activity as *punishment*. While the child might normally *enjoy* written activities, it is possible, through the association of writing with punishment, that a *dislike* for written activities could develop over time.

It is of interest to note the use of classical conditioning in commercial advertising. The pairing of top sports people, leading public figures and exotic places with such wares as toiletries, investment packages and cigarettes to improve sales is classical conditioning at work.

A second type of conditioning was explored by Thorndike, who described the process in the *Law of Effect*, which states that actions followed by pleasurable consequences tend to be *stamped in* while those which lead to unpleasant consequences tend to be *stamped out*. This law provided foundation for a large body of research and theory into operant conditioning, so named since the animal or human being has to *operate* on the environment in order to obtain reinforcement. This research has considered such issues as the effect upon learning (behaviour change) of different types of reinforcer, the effects of delay of reinforcement (the less delay the better) and the effects of scheduling of reinforcement. For example, continuous reinforcement (i.e. the scheduling of reinforcement after every response) gives fastest learning, *but also fastest extinction or "forgetting" of learning*. Where reinforcement is scheduled intermittently, e.g. randomly, or after a fixed number of responses, learning is slower, but so too is extinction. Note the poker machine, or forms of Lotto, for which random schedules of reinforcement operate. Resistance to extinction is very high: there is always the tendency to "have one more go".

Behaviourism and teaching

B.F. Skinner and others have applied these principles to educational practice to produce what is called a *technology* of teaching. This technology involves such procedures as the specification of aims in terms of observable "terminal" or "end product" behaviours, the identification of the "entry behaviour" of the learner, the analysis of what is to be taught into steps small enough to ensure a high level of positive reinforcement, active responding on the part of the learner, the provision of reinforcement as soon as possible after the correct response, and evaluation or feed-back procedures which can detect achievement, or lack of achievement, of the terminal behaviours. The terms *programmed instruction*, *direct instruction* and *behavioural modification* have been applied to this model of teaching. A number of instructional programs based on these principles are available for teachers, e.g. the Distar reading scheme, and Dixon and Engleman's morphographic spelling program.

While Skinner proposed that a significant determinant of behaviour change was external reinforcement, Bandura has argued that much social learning occurs as a result of "vicarious" reinforcement, in a process called *modelling*. In this form of learning, the learner sees a respected model, e.g. a peer in his or her class at school, exhibiting the particular behaviour, and receiving positive reinforcement for such behaviour. The learner, by identifying with the model, receives vicarious satisfaction or reinforcement, which in turn increases the likelihood that the learner will act in future in the same way as the model.

Behaviourist assumptions

Underlying behaviourist psychological theory is a number of assumptions concerning learning and development. The child is assumed to be born *tabula rasa*—like a blank slate—onto which learning is conditioned. The child is viewed as a passive recipient, whose behaviour is *shaped* or determined by external rewards and punishments (in this respect, behaviourism is called a *determinist* theory). The shaping process is incremental, involving the creation of new stimulus-response

The hero of early twentieth-century philosophy!

24

connections. The learning of complex behaviours such as creativity and logical thinking is achieved first by acquiring all of the individual component S-R bonds, and then putting them together. The prime motivation for such learning derives from the environment—that is, extrinsic rewards and punishments. The function of the teacher is to manipulate the learning environment—that is, to schedule reinforcements—in such a way that acquisition of the "terminal" behaviours defined for the educational program occurs as efficiently as possible.

3. THE INTERACTIONIST PERSPECTIVE

Unlike the maturationist view that human behaviour is a product of biology, and the behaviourist that it is primarily a product of environmental influences, the interactionist ideology holds that "man develops to be what he makes himself by his own actions" (Langer, 1969, p. 7). This view of development holds that "Man is a product of his own design . . . Man develops himself from within, not according to a genetic blueprint or environmental dictates but according to self-organisation" (Seaver and Cartwright, 1977, p. 318). While this philosophy recognises that heredity and culture influence development, it views development neither as the unfolding of innately prescribed traits nor the summation of all of the S-R bonds conditioned since birth: the individual plays a *self-determinist* role in his or her own development.

This view of development is inherent in Dewey's "Progressive" educational theory and Piaget's cognitive theory. Piaget proposes that cognitive development involves a change in internal structures, and that these structures, which are essentially rules for processing information and experience, are actively generated by the individual through interaction with the environment. Development results when a mismatch or conflict occurs between these internal mental structures of the learner, and external environmental stimuli (i.e. when a problem has to be solved). When conflict occurs, an internally motivated process called *equilibration* operates to resolve the conflict and, in so doing, the internal structure is modified. This modification of the internal structure constitutes learning. It is for this reason that curricula modelled on Piaget's theory, e.g. Weikart's program at Ypsilanti in Michigan, Lavatelli's teaching kit developed at the University of Illinois, and Kamii's curriculum model all emphasise a problem-centred approach which is designed to challenge the internal cognitive structures of the child.

Underlying Piaget's theory of stages is the *symbolic function*, described by Ginsburg and Opper (1969, p. 73) as follows:

From 2 to 4 years the child begins to develop the ability to make something—a mental symbol, a word, or an object—stand for or represent something else which is not present. For example, the child can use a mental symbol of a bicycle, or the word bicycle or a small schematic toy to stand for the real bicycle when it is not in immediate view.

The ability to create and manipulate symbols to solve problems is the symbolic function. Symbols can take the form of *mental images*—visual, auditory, tactile etc.—which represent objects or events perceived through the senses. Another form of symbol is the *word*, which can represent not only sensory information but also intangible concepts. The child in the *sensory motor* stage does not have the ability to manipulate symbols and "think through" solutions to problems: motor trial and error behaviours must be utilised. The slow development of the ability to manipulate symbols from about two years onwards permits this. However, the solution of problems in a logical manner—using inductive and deductive processes (as distinct from transductive thinking which characterises pre-operational thought)—requires the ability to manipulate symbols in what Piaget calls a *reversible* manner.

This ability to think reversibly develops for most children by about seven or eight years. Until that stage the child is unable to understand, for example, that two balls of clay remain the same in quantity when one is flattened, or that the number of objects remains constant even though arranged differently. Such understanding requires reversibility—the ability in this case to construct sequences of mental symbols representing the ball of clay being flattened, or the objects being rearranged, and to reverse the sequence to "show" the ball or objects in their original states. The relation of reversibility to Piaget's stages is explained as follows:

> The attainment of reversibility and hence logical thought—"operations", in Piaget's language—leads to the stage of development called *concrete operations*. The term "concrete" is applied since the child can think logically only about things that he can sense through sight, touch, smell etc. He cannot deal logically with abstract or intangible ideas. The child of eight years cannot define justice or democracy. He will be able to give concrete examples of justice *in action* but no abstract definition until he reaches what Piaget calls the stage of *formal operations* at about fourteen or fifteen years (Jacka, 1974, pp. 7-8).

Interactionist Theory—implications for teachers

The emphasis on symbolic processes in interactionist theories, such as that of Piaget's, has a number of implications for teachers. If **imagery**, as one of the major tools of thought, develops through the senses, it implies that teachers should provide a rich and stimulating body of *sensory experiences* for children so as to enrich their thinking. Similarly, as **language** is another tool of thought, the child's thinking will be fostered through *a rich language program*. In fact, without language the child cannot reach the stage of formal operations, since the abstract thinking required of that stage can only be carried on through language.

Interactionist theories also place emphasis upon the use of *discovery* teaching-learning procedures. For Piaget, learning occurs when internal mental structures are modified as a result of experience—what he calls *accommodation*. However, the child does not just absorb replicas of experience (as behaviourist theory holds) but, rather, actively modifies such experience as it is internalised in the form of images or other forms of symbol (called *assimilation*). For Piaget, this interplay between assimilation and accommodation is intrinsically motivated and involves the child in personally creating or discovering his or her own unique internal cognitive structures. It is the child who must actively develop such operations as *reversibility, conservation* and *classification*. Expository teaching and direct instruction methods, in which the child is *told* how to conserve, or classify, or think logically, do not, according to Piaget, lead to such operations: the child must *personally* discover ways of processing information and solving problems.

The use of stages

As both the maturational and interactionist theories utilise *stages*, it might be asked whether there is any difference between theories in their *use* of stages. In maturational theory the stages are assumed to be genetically generated and closely age related. Gesell, for example, has stages for the "one year old", the "two year old" and so on, and these represent the unfolding of biologically imprinted characteristics. While psychoanalytic theory does not draw as tight a relation between ages and stages, both Freud and Erikson see increase in age as leading *inexorably* to a new stage, regardless of environmental experience. The purpose of teaching under such a theory is not to produce movement to a *new* stage but to assist the child to successfully master the tasks of the *present* stage. The next stage will occur *regardless* of learning at the previous stage.

Interactionist theory, on the other hand, views cognitive stages as relatively independent of chronological age. The very "bright" child of three might well be able to think in a concrete-operational manner, while a twenty-five year old with mental disability may have difficulty solving sensory-motor tasks. While the stages form an invariate sequence, movement from one to the next is influenced by experience. "For the interactionist, experience is essential to stage progression, and more or richer stimulation leads to faster advance through the series of stages" (Kolberg and Mayer, 1972, p. 459). Unlike the maturational view, "attainment of the next stage is a valid aim of educational experience" under the interactionist ideology (Kolberg and Mayer, 1972, p. 459). To achieve this, the teacher must first identify the cognitive level of the child, then expose the child to forms of reasoning at a level above the child's present stage, presented so as to produce "genuine cognitive and social conflict and disagreement about problematic situations (in contrast to traditional education which has stressed adult 'right answers' and has reinforced 'behaving well')" (Kolberg and Mayer, 1972, p. 459).

*   *   *

A HUMANIST PERSPECTIVE

Any study of psychological theory which underlies educational practice would not be complete without a consideration of humanistic theory. Such theory does not fit readily into one of the three theory groups that have been identified by Kolberg and Mayer, and Seaver and Cartwright. The author's experience in the pre-service and in-service education of teachers suggests that many teachers subscribe to humanistic principles as a basis for their professional practice. It is for that reason that this perspective is introduced now and, in so doing, related to the ideologies so far considered.

Humanistic, or "third force" psychology, is a recent psychology, although its philosophic origins are very old. It was developed in the 1950s very much as a reaction against the existing psychologies, which had proven inadequate as explanations of human motivation and behaviour. Psychoanalytic theory, the "first force", was seen by humanistic psychologists such as Gordon Allport, Abraham Maslow and Carl Rogers as relevant for curing the emotionally neurotic (with whom Freud worked in developing his theory) but inadequate as an explanation of how and why the *healthy* person grows and develops to maturity and fulfilment. Behaviourism (the "second force"), with its focus upon the study of "captive and desperate rats who are primarily concerned with preservation of life" (Frost and Kissinger, 1976, p. 108), was viewed similarly as unable to explain the subtleties and complexities of human learning and motivation. Human learning cannot be segmented into thousands, or millions, of independent stimulus-response connections which, organised into hierarchies, lead to higher human qualities such as creativity, love, dignity and respect for truth. Human behaviour is more than a simple aggregation of S-R bonds. While such analyses might explain the behaviour of lower

28

animals, different assumptions have to be made, and different research strategies followed, to understand human learning.

Humanistic theory views the human being as having an "essential nature" comprising:

> needs, capacities, and tendencies that are in part genetically based, some of which are characteristic of the whole human species, cutting across all cultural lines, and some of which are unique to the individual. These basic needs are on their face good or neutral rather than evil (Maslow, 1970, p. 269).

These needs, which are more psychological than biological, represent the true inner nature of the human being. However, unlike the strong drives proposed by Freud, these motivational forces are assumed to be weak and easily distorted or smothered by an insensitive learning environment.

Maslow identifies a series of needs which form a hierarchy in so far as higher level needs presuppose the satisfaction of needs at *lower* levels. At the most basic level are *physiological* needs—for sleep, exercise, oxygen, and so on. Satisfaction of these needs permits the individual to move to the next level of need—*safety*. If both physiological and safety needs are met, *belongingness* and *love needs* emerge to motivate behaviour. If these needs are satisfied, *esteem needs* become important motivators. All people have a need for "a stable, firmly based, usually high evaluation of themselves, for self-respect, or self-esteem, and for the esteem of others" (Maslow, 1970, p. 45). Inability to satisfy this need leaves the person feeling inadequate, inferior and helpless, a state which Maslow suggests may lead to neurosis.

At the highest level of need is *self-actualisation*—"the desire to become more and more what one idiosyncratically is, to become everything that one is capable of becoming" (Maslow, 1970, p. 46). The postulation of these needs provides an explanation of why, for example, the comfortably retired person will commence a higher degree at the age of seventy, or why the marathon runner will suffer severe privation in order to achieve excellence. In Maslow's words: "A musician must make music, an artist must paint, a poet must write, if he is to be ultimately at peace with himself. What a man *can* be, he *must* be" (1970, p. 46).

Humanistic Theory—implications for teachers

A number of implications for educational practice flow from humanistic theory. The prime goal of education should be *to help the child along the path to self-actualisation*—to a realisation of the child's potentialities. This implies an educational environment which encourages and is supportive of the expression of these potentialities, recognising that they are weak and

Teacher as facilitator—identifying and fostering potentialities.

easily inhibited. The teacher (or *facilitator*, to use Rogers' term) should be sensitive to, and skilled in, the *identification* of these potentialities, and be capable of *fostering* them, once identified. This facilitative role involves helping the child to meet needs at any level of the hierarchy—self-esteem, love and belonging, even safety and physiological needs if deficiency states exist in those areas—for unless these needs are met, evidence of inner potential for growth may not emerge. In fact, Maslow argues that psychopathology "results from a denial, or frustration, or the twisting of man's essential nature" (1970, p. 269).

With regard to teaching methods, humanistic theory places emphasis upon the quality of *interpersonal relationships* that must exist between teacher and learner. Rogers explains as follows:

> The initiation of (significant) learning rests not upon the teaching skills of the leader, not upon scholarly knowledge of the field, not upon curricular planning, not upon the use of audio visual aids, not upon the programmed learning used, not upon lectures and presentations, not upon an abundance of books, though each of these might at one time or another be utilised as an important resource. No, the facilitation of significant learning rests upon certain attitudinal qualities that exist in the personal *relationship* between facilitator and learner. (1983, p. 121)

In expanding on these qualities, Rogers identifies such attitudes as "realness" or genuineness, acceptance, trust, prizing and "empathic understanding" as critical to effective learning.

Humanistic theory also emphasises the use of *discovery methods*. Rogers distinguishes between two general types of learning: meaningless learning, the epitome of which is the

30

memorisation of lists of nonsense syllables (sometimes used by psychologists in learning experiments); and "significant, meaningful, experiential learning". This latter form of learning is characterised by personal involvement. It is self-initiated, *self-discovered* and self-evaluated: "When such learning takes place, the element of meaning to the learner is built into the whole experience" (1983, p. 20).

In terms of the three ideologies considered earlier, humanistic theory is to some extent both maturational and interactionist. The assumption that "needs, capacities, and tendencies" have an innate quality and that the function of the teacher should be to facilitate the expression of these needs represents a link with maturational ideology. On the other hand, the assumption that these needs and capabilities can be easily warped or suppressed by an insensitive educational environment implies a recognition of the interactive relationship between biological and environmental factors. Further, the emphasis upon intrinsic motivation and personal discovery in learning reinforces the link between humanistic and interactionist ideologies.

CONCLUSION

The purpose of this article has been to identify some of the major psychological theories that have relevance for educational practice, and the assumptions that underly them, with a view to providing a framework for teachers to consider the rationales for the curricula and teaching methodologies they use. The author's experience with teachers undertaking in-service courses suggests that while some teachers are "purist" in their commitment to a particular ideology, many are eclectic in that they draw upon more than one ideology. The thesis of this chapter is that there is no one "right" philosophy, or psychological theory, or educational practice. What should be right is the *relationship* between the three.

REFERENCES
Frost, J.L. and Kissinger, J.B. *The Young Child and the Educative Process.* New York, Holt Rinehart and Winston, 1976.
Ginsberg, H. and Opper, S. *Piaget's Theory of Intellectual Development; an introduction.* Englewood Cliffs, Prentice-Hall, 1969.
Jacka, B. *Directions in Primary Education.* Melbourne, Melbourne University Press, 1974.
Kolberg, L. and Mayer, R. "Development as the Aim of Education" in *Harvard Educational Review. 42,* 1972, pp. 449-496.
Langer, J. *Theories of Development.* New York, Holt, Rinehart and Winston, 1969.
Maslow, A.H. *Motivation and Personality.* 2nd edn. New York, Harper and Row, 1970.
Rogers, C. *Freedom to Learn for the 80's.* Columbus, Merrill, 1983.
Seaver, J.W. and Cartwright, C.A. "A Pluralistic Foundation for Training Early Childhood Professionals" in *Curriculum Inquiry. 7,* 1977, pp. 305-328.

THE ROLE OF THE ARTS IN CHILD DEVELOPMENT

June Factor

Institute of Early Childhood Development,
Melbourne College of Advanced Education

> *Poetry is indispensable—if only I knew what for.*
> (Attributed to Jean Cocteau)

In 1981, the Australian Broadcasting Commission presented four thoughtful and stimulating programs by Professor Anthony Barnett, Research Fellow at the Australian National University, titled *Biological Images of Man*. In one of those programs, Professor Barnett played part of an aria from Bellini's opera *Norma*. The unnamed soprano sang with a passionate sadness. Following the music, Professor Barnett asked: "Why do we listen?" (Barnett, 1981).

That is a truly central and significant question for human beings, who are distinguished from other animals in large part, it seems to me, by their engagement in *non-utilitarian activities*—in forms of individual and social behaviour which have no immediately evident practical usefulness. The composition, performance and enjoyment of music, the painting and viewing of pictures, the telling, writing and reading of stories, the design and execution of dance and drama—none of these universal human activities helps to feed, clothe or shelter us. An aria is of no practical use when the roof leaks; no poem can cut bread or tie shoelaces or even stop a lover from leaving. Yet human beings everywhere, and always, have been makers and beneficiaries of what we now call the arts. What functions do these apparently useless phenomena perform in human development and human societies? Should education—in an age of microchip and macro-production, trips to the moon and in-vitro fertilisation, the promise of sunrise industries and the threat of mushroom-cloud sunsets—continue to sponsor and support such seeming fripperies as literature, music, art?

It becomes clear that Barnett's question, and the answers to that question, are of more than academic interest to those of us with some responsibility for the education of the young. There are powerful forces in our community which regard the arts as, at best, a pleasant frill on the body politic, and, at worst, fertile territory for the breeding of the eccentric and the subversive. If we cannot understand, explain and defend the arts and their role in the educative process, then we must expect to see them edged further and further to the periphery, until schools—always factory-like in structure and organisation—succumb completely to the deathly fetish: training for production and consumption of material objects.

A few years ago, a university psychologist wrote to the Melbourne *Herald* with a very clear answer to this question. According to him:

> Books (for children) should contain models of behaviour from which children can learn, models which will show them how to get the good things of life—security, money, a home, a family and happiness.
>
> Books should not be of a fairy tale nature. These only encourage children to daydream, to wish for, hope for one day, but never know how to get some desired object or whatever . . .
>
> It is . . . important to encourage reading for positive gain in today's world. Time is of the essence. Education is the big "medicine" that can cure the ills of society. (Stewart, 1975)

This utilitarian and behaviourist perspective has a very long history. In the 1920s, in post-revolutionary U.S.S.R., the children's poet Kornei Chukovsky was encountering a similar view, espoused by equally rigid gate-keepers of the "commonsense" culture. The poet had gone to a sanatorium in the Crimea, to read to the sick children there. He chose the *Munchausen* fantasy:

> I continued to read the story with the most tender feelings of gratitude to the author, relishing the hearty laughter of my listeners as I read on about the hammer that flew to the moon, the journey on the cannon ball, the horse's legs that were put out to pasture. And whenever I paused for breath the children cried: "Go on! Go on."
>
> Well, that . . . slovenly-looking woman came running up to me . . . she seemed upset and there were red spots of anger all over her face.
>
> "What's this?" she snapped. "What do you think you're doing? We never—it's out of the question!"
>
> She snatched the book out of my hand and looked at it as if it were a frog. She carried it off holding it gingerly with two fingers, while the children howled with disappointment . . .
>
> Then there appeared a young man in some kind of uniform and both began to speak to me as if I were a thief whom they had caught red-handed:
>
> "What right do you have to read this trash to our children?"
>
> And the young man went on to explain, in an instructor's tone, that books for Soviet children must not be fantasies, not fairy tales, but only the kind that offer most authentic and realistic facts.

Chukovsky attempted to expound the value of fantasy stories, but his explanation fell on deaf ears. Later he reflected:

> Protecting little ones from folk songs, tall tales, fairy tales, these people are hardly aware of the banal fetish they make of practicality. As a result, they look upon every children's book as something that must immediately produce some visible, touchable, beneficial effect, as if a book were a nail or a yoke. They thus reveal the pettiness and the narrowness of their Philistine thinking ... Why are these peculiar people so convinced ... that radio and *The Little Humpbacked-Horse* are so incompatible? Why do they think that if a child reads this fairy tale he will most certainly turn away from technology and will henceforth daydream about firebirds to the end of his days? How did they arrive at this categorical position—*either* the fairy tale *or* the dynamotor? As if the most uninhibited fantasy and imagination were not needed for the inventing of the dynamotor! Fantasy is the most valuable attribute of the human mind and it should be diligently nurtured from earliest childhood. (Chukovsky, 1963, pp. 115-117, 125)

If we accept Chukovsky's argument, then part of the answer to Barnett's question lies in the human need, the human hunger to make sense of the world. In order to understand their experiences and their environment, children use their *imagination*, that remarkable human faculty which enables us to look ahead, to wonder, to pretend, to think "What if . . .?". Without this faculty there would be no science, no technology—and none of the arts. (The story may be apocryphal, but it is said that Albert Einstein, confronted by an anxious and ambitious mother who asked for advice concerning the best way to rear her young son to become a great scientist, paused, thought a moment, and then replied: "Madam, read him fairy tales." "Yes?" gasped the surprised mother. "And what else?" "More fairy tales," said Einstein firmly.) As Chukovsky declared:

> The present belongs to the sober, the cautious, the routine-prone, but the future belongs to those who do not rein in their imagination. (Chukovsky, 1963, p. 124)

This view of human development stresses the *necessity* for an imaginative life in order that the child is enabled to grow emotionally and intellectually. It suggests that artists—the makers and doers of the arts—exist as part of the normal and essential continuum of human experience, reflection, expression and action.

The concept of the arts *as intrinsic to human life* gains support from the studies of the English psychoanalyst D.W. Winnicott. Educated as a Freudian analyst, Winnicott in the 1950s and 60s grew uneasy that "cultural experience has not found its true place in the theory used by analysts in their work and in their thinking". Painstakingly, he set out to explore and explain the existence of certain universal features of human life: play in childhood, and the arts and religion in adult life. He developed an intriguing theory that linked the infant's attachment to thumb or blanket with his or her later special relationship with other external objects. Winnicott argued that the young child finds in these "transitional objects" a "defence against anxiety", and that as he or she grows older, these transitional phenomena diffuse into wider activity: play, dreaming, religion and the arts.

> There is a direct development from transitional phenomena to playing, and from playing to shared playing, and from this to cultural experiences . . . The transitional phenomena represent the early stages of the use of illusion. (Winnicott, 1974)

Winnicott recognised the special qualities of the arts which are common also to children's play: the temporary separation from the exterior world of objects and the interior world of thought and feeling; the autonomy and freedom available in this "intermediate zone" ("I'm the king of the castle!"; the transformations in *Swan Lake*); and the exploration of experience indirectly, through symbols (the child's drawing of Mummy, the Aboriginal kangaroos and fish on ancient cave walls, Picasso's *Guernica*). Above all, he stressed the indispensability of play and the arts for the healthy growth of individuals, for expressive and joyful growth.

From a rather different perspective, a number of literary theorists have come to very similar conclusions. In the 1920s, the English critic Percy Lubbock commented:

> We are continually piecing together our fragmentary evidence about the people around us and moulding their images in thought. It is the way in which we make our world; partially, imperfectly, very much at haphazard, but still perpetually, everybody deals with his experience like an artist. (Lubbock, 1954, p. 7)

The same point was made by Barbara Hardy in 1975, when she declared that:

> Narrative imagination is a common human possession, differentiating us, as Isocrates insisted, from the animals, and enabling us to "come together and found cities and make laws and invent arts . . ." Narrative is crucial, in life and in literature. Our ordinary and our extraordinary day depend on the stories we hear. One piece of news, a change of intention, even a revision of memory, a secret, a disclosure, a piece of gossip may change our lives.

Hardy linked the apparently generic human characteristics of dreaming and day-dreaming with our everyday "storying"— jokes, gossiping, imagining—and with the conscious structuring of narrative forms in the novel:

> Day-dreams and author have in common the decision to pretend and the knowledge that it is pretence. They also share the sense of contact with the other world from which we depart and to which we

return . . . We tell stories in order to escape from the stubbornness of identity. (Hardy, 1975)

Such views emphasise the "artist" in everyone. They suggest that it is false and misleading to polarise reality and fantasy: we are as needful of the psychological and intellectual stimulus and nourishment provided by the arts as of bread and a secure roof. The small boy running with his arms outstretched, mimicking the noise of an aeroplane engine, is simultaneously plane, pilot, crew and passengers. His is the largely undifferentiated creativity of early childhood, the whole-hearted involvement of body and mind in the imaginative enterprise of the moment. But even quite young children show an awareness of the possibilities of a range of artistic devices. The dictated letter of a four-year-old girl demonstrates a skilful playing with words, ideas and sounds, inventive juxtapositions, and a firm grasp of the concept of an audience:

Dear Amber,
   You could come to my birthday. Purple green spots and yellow green spots and jugglers jugglers won't you have a juggle? Juggle juggle ice-cream cones, won't you juggle ice-cream cones? Throw rocks in the sky, they go down to the ground. Boats are going upside down in the water. Books are going book to books, book to books to books. Cones are dancing in the circus. Pens are dancing in the air. Big tables are floating in the ground and lamps are turning on and off. Bookshelves are crying. Bees are dancing in the garden, they're going up and down. Keep your eyes shut and you'll go bounce, bounce, bounce and the air is floating and rocks are getting chipped off and people are ouching and covers are groaning and cats and boys are whinging and dogs are woofing and cats are sitting at the doorstep turning their backs over. Lollies don't want to be eaten and doors are knocking and shores are going twister twister twister and magic makes things. Won't you have a lolly in your mouth?

This lyrical prose-poem (from my own personal correspondence) suggests that very young humans are already resourceful "performers", who utilise words (and body movements, pleasing sounds and visual forms) with "a sense of game, of playfulness" (Josipovici, 1977, p. 122). Such playfulness gives them the freedom to experiment and, at the same time, protects them from charges of "getting it wrong" or "you can't do it that way". In stories, poems, songs, dances and pictures, ice-creams can be juggled and bookshelves and lollies have volition. There is a delicious *power* for the maker and the performer, of particular significance for the young, who are often made acutely conscious of their ignorance and powerlessness. When Chukovsky's twenty-three month old daughter, having only recently learnt that cats *meow*, dogs *bow-wow* and roosters go *kukuruku*, approached her father one day with the words: "Daddy, 'oggie—meow!'" he responded with the realis-

36

"... the indispensibility of play and the arts for the healthy
growth of individuals, for expressive and joyful growth."

tic: "No . . . the doggie bow-wows". The little girl insisted laughingly: " 'Oggie—meow!" When finally Chukovsky joined in her game and said: "And the rooster meows!" the child was delighted. She had made a joke, she had played a game, and she had led her father through it! Chukovsky observed that young children are dedicated to these "topsy-turvies" in play and in the arts because such absurdities reinforce their sense of reality (Chukovsky, 1963, pp. 97-8). I would go further and point to the way in which they offer children the rare opportunity to construct and control a situation, to lead rather than follow, teach as well as learn.

Evidence that this playful and purposeful creative exploration is at the very core of childhood can be drawn from another, bleaker source. Together with the ashes, the mounds of shoes, hair and false teeth, the blank staring eyes of the survivors, we have a record from at least one Nazi concentration camp written and sketched by its inmates—its youngest inmates. At Terezin in Czechoslovakia, almost 15,000 Jewish children under the age of fifteen spent weeks, months or years with their families in the crowded barracks. Only 100 children survived the hunger, brutality and the planned extermination camp at Oswiecim. Yet, thanks to the resourceful adults who smuggled in paper and pencils to Terezin, the children were able to record their memories, hopes, dreams and nightmare fears in poems and drawings (Volavkova, 1978).

When dewdrops sparkle in the grass
And earth's aflood with morning light,
A blackbird sings upon a bush
To greet the dawning after night.
Then I know how fine it is to live.

(From "Birdsong")

We'll sail a long, long way
And dreams will turn to truth.
Oh, how sweet the name Morocco!
Listen!
Now it's time.

(From "To Olga")

The sun has made a veil of gold
So lovely that my body aches.
Above, the heavens shriek with blue
Convinced I've smiled by some mistake.
The world's abloom and seems to smile.
I want to fly but where, how high?
If in barbed wire, things can bloom
Why couldn't I? I will not die!

(From "On A Sunny Evening")

38

For seven weeks I've lived in here,
Penned up inside this ghetto
But I have found my people here.
The dandelions call to me
And the white chestnut candles in the court.
Only I never saw another butterfly.

That butterfly was the last one.
Butterflies don't live in here,
In the ghetto.

(From "The Butterfly")

The heaviest wheel rolls across our foreheads
To bury itself deep somewhere inside our memories.

(From "Terezin")

Somewhere, far away out there,
Childhood sweetly sleeps . . .

(From "Terezin")

It is impossible to contemplate the scraps of children's writing and drawing salvaged from the Terezin camp without recognising how remarkable, and how tenacious, is the human urge to express feelings, thoughts and wishes imaginatively, to share the pulsing of the private heart. We begin to understand the poet Osip Mandelstam, who said: "Words are sheer pleasure, a cure for anguish" (Mandelstam, 1975, p. 320). In the midst of desolation and fear, the arts gave these children some respite, some autonomy and freedom. Their humanity speaks to us, they assert their humanity through their drawings and poems.

If the arts are central to the experience of every individual, they are perhaps even more crucial for the bonding and connecting which make social life possible. We acknowledge this readily when we observe an Aboriginal corroboree or a New Guinea sing-sing; our ethnocentricity may make us a little slower to discern the same processes of shared participation and pleasure in creative performance in an audience at a symphony concert, a country and western jamboree, or an exhibition of paintings. Every society has developed an extraordinary range of art forms that delight, and unite, large or small groups within a community. It is a fundamental way in which we all participate in what one writer has called "the conversation of mankind" (Oakeshott, 1959). We listen to a song and are transported (an old but apt expression) to the world and mood evoked by the music; we read a novel and vicariously share the experiences of its characters—while simultaneously reflecting on their lives, and our own. Children, from the safety of an arm-

39

chair or a warm lap, may adventure into the world like Max in Maurice Sendak's *Where The Wild Things Are*:

> *That very night in Max's room a forest grew*
> *and grew—*
> *and grew until his ceiling hung with vines*
> *and the walls became the world all around*
> *and an ocean tumbled by with a private boat for Max*
> *and he sailed off through night and day*
> *and in and out of weeks*
> *and almost over a year*
> *to where the wild things are—*

returning, like Max, with a smile and the confident certainty that monsters can and will be tamed. In the words of the author of *The Necessity of Art*, man (used generically) has a continuing need to

> absorb the surrounding world and make it his own; to extend his inquisitive, world-hungry "I" in science and technology as far as the remotest constellations and as deep as the innermost secrets of the atom; to unite his limited "I" in art with a communal existence; to make his individuality *social* . . . Art is the indispensable means for this merging of the individual with the whole. It reflects his infinite capacity for association, for sharing experience and ideas (Fischer, 1963, pp. 8-9).

Cassirer called man "an *animal symbolicum* . . . symbolic thought and symbolic behavior are among the most characteristic features of human life" (Cassirer, 1967, p. 27). The arts use symbolic modes to offer alternative templates, multitudinous ways of shaping and ordering experience. They catch the endless, changing flux of life and give it shape, and meaning, and some permanence. We are surrounded by chaos, says Kermode, "and equipped for co-existence with it only by our fictive powers" (Kermode, 1967, p. 64). The most painful, tragic experience is transformed, through art, into forms which appear to give the artist (and audience) control, and hence power. "It is a profound saying that 'all sorrows can be borne if you can put them into a story', but what it means is that all sorrows can be borne if we can succeed in substituting poetic images in their place" (Oakeshott, 1959, p. 48). The artist "selects . . . detects . . . significance, he disengages and throws aside whatever is accidental and meaningless . . . he liberates and completes" (Lubbock, 1954, p. 18).

We all, children included, cannot survive without the shaping and patterning of the arts; they make possible our understanding of the world, our contemplation of its fearsome chaos, and the intermittent confidence in our ability to survive and rejoice.

REFERENCES

Barnett, Anthony. "Biological Images of Man", *Science Show 18 & 19*. Sydney, Australian Broadcasting Commission, 1981.

Cassirer, Ernst. *An Essay on Man*. Yale University Press, 1967 (first published 1944).

Chukovsky, Kornei. *From Two to Five*. Brisbane, Jacaranda Press, 1963 (first published 1925).

Fischer, Ernst. *The Necessity of Art: A Marxist Approach*. London, Penguin, 1963.

Hardy, Barbara. *Tellers and Listeners; the narrative imagination*. London, Athlone Press, 1975.

Josipovici, Gabriel. *The Lessons of Modernism and Other Essays*. London, Macmillan, 1977.

Kermode, Frank. *The Sense of Ending: studies in the theory of fiction*. New York, Oxford University Press, 1967.

Lubbock, Percy. *The Craft of Fiction*. London, Cape, 1954 (first published 1921).

Mandelstam, Nadezhda. *Hope Against Hope*. London, Penguin, 1975.

Oakeshott, Michael. *The Voice of Poetry in the Conversation of Mankind*. London, Bowes & Bowes, 1959.

Sendak, Maurice. *Where The Wild Things Are*. New York, Harper and Row, 1963.

Stewart, Warren. "Help Your Child to Read". Melbourne, *Herald* (newspaper), 16 October 1975.

Volavkova, Hana (ed.). . . . *I never saw another butterfly; Children's Drawings and Poems from Terezin Concentration Camp*. New York, Schocken Books, 1978.

Winnicott, D.W. *Playing and Reality*. London, Penguin, 1974.

THE EDUCATION OF THE INTELLECTUALLY HANDICAPPED CHILD

Brian McKeown
Karonga House Public School,
Epping (N.S.W.)

INTRODUCTION

For many people the subject of handicap is only thought of in terms of wheelchairs and white canes. Others may see mental retardation as the only real handicap and the only real manifestation of that is the institution. But the question of handicap and the handicapped is one of extreme complexity and perplexity. Worldwide estimates put the number of people who exhibit some form of handicap between 500 and 600 millions. In Australia the latest figures show that some 35,000 students are receiving a service in special schools and classes (Andrews, 1976). In N.S.W. there are 3,500 moderately/severely intellectually handicapped children requiring services from the government system. These figures do not include children who are receiving a service from Youth and Community Schools, voluntary associations and church schools. At present there are 73 special schools in N.S.W. whose sizes range from as few as six pupils to as many as 180. Staffing can vary from one teacher and a teacher's aide to combined staffing in excess of seventy personnel, including as many as ten separate disciplines and specialist teachers.

Logically, the removal of an intellectually handicapped child from the regular classroom implies that that child has failed to cope with even the low status knowledge of the regular curriculum. What, therefore, do we offer a child who cannot compete with his or her normal peers? Some would see an alternative curriculum as being negative in the sense that it will offer non-knowledge—the so-called hidden curriculum consisting mainly of the development of social skills and the

42

modification of behaviour. Fortunately this is not (at least should not) be regarded as the sole service delivered to the intellectually handicapped child. Teachers in Special Schools and classes offer their pupils a wide range of activities and subjects designed to help each child to realise his or her greatest potential. In spite of the best intentions, dedication and skill the teacher brings to the child, however, these must be weighed against the social effects of isolation from his or her normal peers. *This is the fundamental issue at stake in the education of the intellectually handicapped child.*

WHO ARE THE INTELLECTUALLY HANDICAPPED?
There are few areas of education that have managed to present more stereotypes than that of Special Education. The most popular misconception of the intellectually handicapped child is that he or she belongs to a homogeneous group. The intellectually handicapped child may bring to the classroom a vast array of disabilities, not the least of which may be intellectual handicap. The N.S.W. Department of Education recognises three major categories of intellectual handicap. The major criteria for categorisation is I.Q. level.

(a) The Mildly Intellectually Handicapped
Children whose I.Q. ranges between 55 and 80—euphemistically called Opportunity A (O.A.). Some 22,400 such children are recognised in the N.S.W. education system. They are catered for in seven Special Schools and 365 Special Classes in regular schools. Two schools serve as residentials. Class sizes range to 15 pupils.

(b) The Moderately Intellectually Handicapped
Children whose I.Q. is in the range 30-55—dubbed Opportunity F (O.F.). N.S.W. figures show that 13 Special Schools enrol such pupils, whilst 61 classes are in regular schools. Class size is one teacher to nine pupils.

(c) The Severely Intellectually Handicapped
Children whose I.Q. is assessed as being 30 minus. This group also includes the multiple handicapped child, who may have as many as six major handicaps *other* than that of intellectual disability. There are 46 N.S.W. Department of Education schools catering for these children, whilst four regular schools are committed to the provision of a service. Schools that have previously catered only for the O.A. and O.F. child are being increasingly committed to the enrolment of pupils who fall within this category. Class size is one teacher to nine pupils.

PROVISION OF SERVICES
Non-government Schools
There are currently 34 non-government schools catering for the needs of almost 600 severely intellectually handicapped children. These schools do not compete with, but rather complement, the Departmental services. The degree of cooperation and exchange of ideas and resources between government and non-government schools is very high and is a most commendable feature of the overall pattern of services available to the intellectually handicapped child.

Commonwealth Schools Commission
For those children for whom no suitable service is available in schools, the Commonwealth has embarked upon a program of service provision. Twenty-one programs are currently funded and provide educational and developmental services for 340 severely intellectually handicapped children. The number of children in these programs range from as few as one child to as many as 160.

The N.S.W. Government has committed itself to the provision of an educational service for all children in N.S.W. Although this in itself is a commendable feature, the process of developing suitable and adequate support and delivery services to meet the unique needs of a range of intellectually handicapped children has yet to be overcome.

WHAT TO TEACH?
There is no single methodology or philosophy that can serve the educational requirements of all intellectually handicapped children. Furthermore, the question of what should be taught to the intellectually handicapped child, in order that he or she can best cope with future environments, is one that is difficult to resolve. For better or worse, much of what we teach the child is based upon immediate needs and there is a general failure to look at the child's needs beyond the classroom. Special education has generally eschewed theoretical issues such as *why* we do things, in favour of *what* to do. Thus we can find adolescents still attempting to cope with beginning readers, inset puzzles and grappling with the comprehension of a Dick Bruna book.

Although few would argue that the intellectually handicapped child requires the support of extra personnel and oft times sophisticated resources in order to enhance educational and developmental ability, these are not automatically forthcoming. Resources are not only limited but spread unequally throughout the State. There can be no doubt that one of the most disturbing features of Special Education is the growth of an ever-widening gap in availability of resources to schools.

44

Thus there is a growing elitism within the schools offering services to the intellectually handicapped. This elitism is reflected not only in those basic requirements, such as adequate staffing and essentials such as availability of toilets and tissues, but in sophisticated resources such as heated indoor therapy pools, provision of buses and well-stocked toy libraries and audio-visual equipment. This problem can only be overcome by ensuring that all intellectually handicapped children have access to a range of equipment and personnel that is considered essential in order to implement worthwhile programs. To date, much of what we teach the child has been based upon available resources rather than upon the unique needs of the individual.

The determination of what best to teach the intellectually handicapped child, as mentioned earlier, poses great difficulty for educators. It is clear that watered down versions of the regular curriculum may prove inadequate in meeting the needs of the wide range of intellectually handicapped children. Furthermore, even curricula developed for the mildly intellectually handicapped and the moderately intellectually handicapped are not practical for the severely intellectually handicapped. To date, much of what is taught to the O.A. and O.F. child is of a remedial nature with an emphasis upon basic skills in the three R's. Such a developmental approach to education, however, will have to be examined closely in view of post school placement for these children. The ability of the O.A. and the O.F. child to cope with present and future environments cannot be guaranteed under the narrow dimensions of present curricula based upon remediation. There needs to be a widening of approaches to include such matters as work skills, use of recreation and leisure, sexuality, transportation, money management etc.—all matters which will relate directly to the quality of life of the intellectually handicapped. Although a great deal of research has shown that much can be learned by

45

intellectually handicapped children, and that till now we have underestimated their ability to learn, the real problem arises when we attempt to translate these ideals without adequate resources and personnel. At this stage it may be worthwhile to survey briefly a number of issues which promise to affect the quality of learning now available to the intellectually handicapped child.

EARLY INTERVENTION

Increasing attention is being focused upon the value of early intervention programs in effecting the education of the intellectually handicapped child. It is recognised that the experiences of any child in the first five years of development is crucial in determining educational progress. Such programs include gross motor skills such as body positioning, visual and auditory stimulation; fine motor skills including such activities as reaching and grasping, object manipulation and visual motor; communication skills and simple self-help and social skills such as eating, drinking etc. Apart from the more obvious developmental value of this type of program, there is an added gain in that, by enhancing skills, the child may be more readily accepted into the regular classroom.

Although a number of programs are in operation, they tend to be scattered and uncoordinated. They are all too often based upon limited funding and are of limited duration. There appears to be little coordination between such programs that do operate and schools to which the child may later enter.

Although there is provision for special pre-school classes for the deaf, blind and physically handicapped, little attempt has been made to provide adequate services for the intellectually handicapped pre-school child. The present move to enrol these children in special schools from the age of three is commendable, but cannot make up for the time already lost. One of the ironies of Special Education is the fact that the mildly intellectually handicapped (or O.A.) child cannot enter classes so designated until the age of eight years.

CURRICULUM FOR SEVERELY INTELLECTUALLY HANDICAPPED CHILDREN

It would be fair to say that the entry of children with severe intellectual handicap has occurred before either the teachers or the technology were available. There is no doubt that these children, often displaying a number of profound handicapping conditions such as blindness, deafness, extreme forms of behaviour, lack of any form of communication and locomotion skills and perhaps a brittle medical background, provide the greatest challenge to our teachers.

It is a measure of the N.S.W. Department of Education's concern towards providing an adequate service for these children that it has established a curriculum team to develop a statement relating to the many unique problems that such children bring to the classroom. For this curriculum the accepted meaning of education may have to be redefined in order that a legitimacy be given to those activities that are not part of so-called normal and modified curriculums. Unlike other curriculums, this one will be based upon the needs of the child rather than a subject. It will include such areas as toilet training, feeding, behaviour management, communication skills and locomotion. The Project Committee has recognised the need to enlist the services of a wide range of disciplines in the educational development of the severely intellectually handicapped child. Such recognition is both commendable and logical.

STRATEGIES AND INITIATIVES FOR SPECIAL EDUCATION IN N.S.W.

The above report, chaired by Dr Pat Doherty, Director of the N.S.W. Division of Guidance and Special Education, was commissioned by the N.S.W. Minister for Education in 1980. Its release in 1982 promised to have a significant effect upon the organisation and availability of services for the handicapped child in N.S.W. schools. It recognised that Special Education was not a mere adjunct of education generally but a specific service that could not be efficiently endorsed without resort to trained personnel and specialised resources. The report examined all areas of Special Education, including groups in need, teacher preparation, curricula, parent involvement, integration and toy libraries etc. In all, it made 479 recommendations regarding future directions in Special Education. Some 58 such recommendations related to teacher training alone. In spite of widespread approval and acclamation by both government and other organisations, no attempt has yet been made to implement any of the recommendations. Like Mr Curdle's treatise, the *Strategies and Initiatives* document could well turn out to be a literary curiosity, well received at the time, but which offered a kind of catharsis rather than change.

MULTI-DISCIPLINARY APPROACH

There is general agreement that, in order to deliver the most effective service to the intellectually handicapped child, we need to enlist the help of specialist personnel. Such personnel belong not only to the teaching profession but also to such professions as Speech Therapy, Occupational Therapy and Physiotherapy. Nurses and Social Workers are examples of other professionals who might be included in a multi-disciplinary team. Naturally, such a team would also include the parent, guardian or advocate of the child. In spite of the

47

best intentions, however, there is very little evidence of this type of approach being viable under the present staffing ratios in the Special School. Only very limited support is available, for example, in therapy areas, whilst the existence of nurses, social workers etc. in N.S.W. schools is purely academic at this stage.

The multi-disciplinary approach to special education is all too often advocated by those who have no real idea of the many complicated issues involved in the administration of a class and a school for intellectually handicapped children. For some reason best known to themselves, they fail to appreciate the enormous task that the class teacher is attempting to cope with in the here and now. Once we carve our way through the mystique and terminology associated with the intellectually handicapped child, we come to the reality of one teacher attempting to cope with the individual needs of at least nine severely to mildly intellectually handicapped children. Such a teacher may or may not have a teacher's aide. How such a teacher is suddenly going to have the time (and obviously the host of new skills) required to effectively direct and maintain cohesiveness with a group of other professionals must be resolved. Certainly such an approach, for all its merits, cannot operate under the existing model.

THE FUTURE OF EDUCATION FOR THE INTELLECTUALLY HANDICAPPED CHILD

Children who present a degree of developmental disability and learning difficulties now account for 18% of the school population. The obvious costs in implementing suitable programs for such a large and various group of children will be extremely high and involves a degree of complexity not yet faced by educators and governments in Australia. Although there has been a moral commitment to provide adequate facilities for all handicapped children, including the severely intellectually handicapped, such a commitment must receive the support of a wide range of personnel and equipment. To date, the provision of such services (in N.S.W. at least) has depended more upon the ability of particular groups, including schools, to agitate, rather than upon the use of a recognised formula that will ensure a reasonable degree of service and resources for all handicapped children. There has been little attempt to realise the difficulties faced by teachers in their attempts to implement programs, particularly those teachers working with severe and profoundly multiple handicapped children. The intellectually handicapped child has fared worst in the provision of services to the handicapped child in general. What conclusions can be drawn from the fact that if a child is blind he or she will be placed in a class of two whereas if a

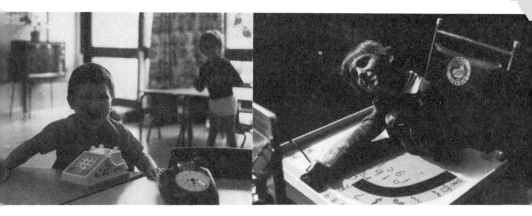

child is blind and intellectually handicapped he or she will be placed in a class of nine?

Today, many children who began their education in Special Schools are reaching leaving age. What will now happen to these children? In a time that has seen the encroachment of more able young people into sheltered workshops, taking the place of intellectually handicapped youths who might normally fill such positions, and far too few Activity Centres for the severely intellectually handicapped, serious consideration must be given to extending school leaving ages. Admittedly, this is only a stop-gap measure, but can we continue to justify the amount of resources already provided for these children in schools by allowing them to spend the rest of their lives in institutions?

Ironically, the Transition Education Scheme, which has provided the Special School with limited degrees of extra staffing and resources to enable them to find post school placement for a number of their pupils, has been abandoned. So far there has been no commitment under the Participation Equity Program to include all intellectually handicapped children under the replacement scheme.

Finally, professional involvement in Special Education has been marked by tensions and conflicts of interest. If we are to provide the handicapped child with the best possible service, professional interests must give way to a greater understanding of the roles of others and how those roles might be best used in the determination of such a service.

REFERENCES

Andrews, R.J. et al., A Survey of Special Education in Australia; provision, needs and priorities in the education of children with handicaps and learning difficulties. Fred and Eleanor Schonell Education Research Centre, University of Queensland, 1979.

Doherty, P.J. (Chairperson), Strategies and Initiatives for Special Education in N.S.W.; a report of the working party on a plan for Special Education in N.S.W. May, 1982.

N.S.W. Department of Education, Statewide Service Pattern—3rd Term 1983. Intellectually Handicapped Program.

Children and
literacy learning

BEGINNING LITERACY LEARNING

Garth H. Brown
Language and Media Department
Phillip Institute of Technology (Vic.)

Donald Graves (1978, p. 10) claims that children want to write before they want to read: "They are more fascinated by their own marks than the marks of others. Young children leave their messages on refrigerators, wallpaper, moist window panes, sidewalks and even on paper".

Children believe they can write, yet are often unsure about their capacity to read (Walshe, 1981, p. 9). A recent local study of the literacy development of eighteen pre-school children supports this claim.* Dunstall (1983) found that all children could write something when asked even though the initial response by two of the children to the question: "Can you write?" was a firm "No!" All children selected a pen and paper and were pleased to demonstrate their "writing". Yet when asked: "Can you read?" only six of the children replied affirmatively and in some of these instances the response was not particularly accurate when compared to some children who answered "No!" In fact, many of the children who replied "No" were using more effectively reading type behaviours such as book handling skills and identification of children's names. It is interesting to note that *all* children could recognise at least some black and white photocopies of logos such as *McDonalds*, *Coca Cola*, *Kit Kat* and *Omo* either by the precise name or functionally. For example, *Kit Kat* was identified as "a kind of chocolate" and *Omo* was read as "what you wash the clothes with".

---

* Dunstall's naturalistic study of 18 kindergarten children (7 girls and 11 boys) was carried out at Newlands Pre-School Centre located in Coburg, a northern suburb of Melbourne, in mid 1982. Home languages included Spanish, Dutch, Philippino, Italian, Greek, Croatian, Lebanese and English.

The children of this study believed that they could write and they demonstrated this ability. A much smaller percentage believed they could read and, overall, there was confusion about what might constitute reading. Yet all children could identify at least some black and white photocopies of logos and many could identify their own names and the names of others.

Perhaps this confidence in writing and uncertainty with reading tells more about children's perceptions (many of which emanate from adults) about what reading is than of their capabilities in reading. (Not that such perceptions are unimportant, particularly motivationally.) A child believes that writing a line or two of scribble, or a letter of the alphabet, or a shape similar to a letter is "real" writing and we as adults often support the result as a valid communicative act, as we do with young children's early oral language attempts.

In reading, the situation may be somewhat different. Even though a child may be able to recognise his/her name, or the label on a *Coca Cola* bottle or the STOP sign (activities analogous to those described in writing), these capabilities are not often recognised as "reading". In the supermarket, the selection of a packet of *Weeties* by a child of 3½ is simply part of shopping, not reading. Adults do not often indicate that such behaviour *is* reading. By contrast, as much as a child's few lines of scribble, a letter or a group of letters or shapes is accepted and acknowledged as writing. But reading the *Coca Cola* label on a bottle, or calling out: "There's *McDonald's*", even if tied to some degree to the logo's shape and its environment, seems to me to be "reading" just as much as scribble or a few printed shapes are "writing".

Even when a child picks up a book and "reads" the pictures or "talks the story" as he/she turns the pages, there may be a greater inclination amongst adults to say that this is not really reading. This partly explains the tendency for children to be reticent and unsure about their reading rather than their writing.

READING AND WRITING: PARALLEL DEVELOPMENT?

Perhaps then, despite children's apparent feelings about their literacy learnings, their actual capabilities and their progress in reading and writing (at least for many children) is reasonably parallel. To show what I mean, let us look at Ben's literacy learning from pre-school to Grade 1, the grade he is in currently. Ben (aged 4.3 at 1 January) is one of the children of Dunstall's research. Does his progress in reading and writing seem reasonably parallel despite his eagerness to write and his reticence about reading? What can be outlined of his literacy learning?

Ben's Reading

In answer to the question: "Can you read?", Ben replied: "Sort of!", which proved to be an insightful response. He identified by name eleven of thirty photocopied, black and white logos, plus another nine with a functional equivalent, such as stating for the *White Wings* logo the word "flour". He also identified four of the logos when they were presented in hand-written form. The numbers to ten, but with confusion on six and nine, certain letters, three names of children, including his own, were also identified. He knows where to begin and how to proceed when "reading" a book, knows the function of print and can select a word. When demonstrating his "reading" Ben tended to indicate letters and words already known.

Ben's Writing

When asked if he could write and if he could demonstrate, Ben replied, "Yes!" and proceeded to write the following:

BHe ΛF
BEN
ND|FFO
~~ΩEB~~
BEΛυMΛ
~~BH~~
BAT/MAΛ

(At an earlier stage he'd written his name as ΛMJΩƎB .)

Ben has clear notions of uniformity, line and direction, at least within words when writing. In July and August he dictated his story sentences and requested they be written under his pictures. In September he began to label his pictures by requesting a copy of the words needed. This practice of labelling his drawings himself by copying continued for the remainder of the kindergarten (pre-school) year, but included some requests for sentences for copying.

Ben's progress in reading and writing at this stage seems to be reasonably parallel. He clearly understands that written language conveys messages and that one can read and write such messages. He knows certain elementary book handling skills and writes with evidence of line, uniformity and direction at the word level. In reading, directionality was confined to general book handling; that is, Ben did not seem aware of direction within lines of print. He identified particular words, letters and numbers in his general environment and in books. He was able to write certain letters, numbers and words, label his pictures by copying supplied words and at times he requested sentences for copying. He tended not to invent spellings when writing nor did he seem to use grapho-phonics as a source of information when endeavouring to read.

In May the following year, however, Ben at school was writing in this way:

Ty let me play with his car.

And at home:

I brought a three cars to school.

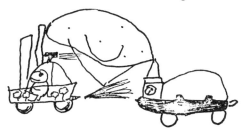

(Assistance was requested from Mum with the word "school". Through questioning, Ben supplied "sk". Double "o" was given, then he added "L".)

55

At this time, he was reading from the series *Reading 360* and he read *Here is Ben* (McDonald & Woodroffe, 1976), a basal reader of sixteen pages with a vocabulary of twenty-nine different words. Ben was able to identify nine words: *Ben, can, is, said, Mum, Dad, run, we* and *you*.

By early June, a year later (Grade 1), Ben's writing had become more sophisticated:

IN 1983 my fale got a cemPetA
I wes IN geD pep
I weD to scttool wef my mum
and my Bevve
I HeD A cABBe Hes Bet ro in 1984
it t is not ter

In 1983 my family got a computer.
I was in grade prep.
I walked to school with my mum and my brother.
I had a cubby house but in 1984 it is not there.

In early July Ben was asked to read Lorraine Wilson's *Magpies* (Nelson, Country Kids 2) but found it difficult to read without support. He later read *The Blanket* by John Burningham (Cape) and made the following miscues:

Blan-ket (Re-stated appropriately by the adult listening to Ben's reading.)

THE BLANKET

When I go to bed

(Eventually given the word "always" by the listener.)

I/always take my blanket   *away*

One night

I could not find   *Called no*

my blanket.

My ^ Mummy looked

in the bathroom.

Daddy looked

in the cupboard.

And I looked

under my bed.

But we could not

find the blanket.

Some Mummys
So Mummy looked

ⓒ *wassing*
in the washing.

And Daddy looked

ⓒ *a*
in the car.

ⓒ *fie*
But I found the blanket

under my pillow

I
and ^ went to sleep.

Not that such a brief outline is considerable evidence (far from it), but Ben's progress in reading and writing, over almost three years, does seem to be reasonably parallel, even though in Kindergarten (pre-school) he was more eager to write than to read.

There's still some tendency, apparently, to ask for words in writing ("When you can't write it, ask your Mum") whereas in reading, when difficulties arise, Ben not only claims he would ask Mum but stated: "I'd think about it, what it might be". Despite his protestation that he would ask Mum for help (which is a reasonable strategy) he seems now to be quite actively exploring and analysing the written word. Dyson (1982, p. 831) would in fact claim that this is essential: "To become literate, the child must focus on and analyse language itself".

Ben is clearly more successful now at thinking "what it might be" (that is, exploring and analysing when writing) than he was a year ago. His invented spellings, used to the degree when adults can read the writing with some confidence, began to appear consistently around early Grade 1. Whether all children will move through an overt invented spelling stage remains to be clarified. But children who begin to use, in their writing, their knowledge of the sounds in our language, allied with their growing knowledge of the graphic symbols used in writing, appear to be making a significant advance. For one thing, the child can begin to read his/her own writing which must be beneficial for literacy development. (See Butler & Turbill, 1984, pp. 19 and 20.)

In his oral reading of *The Blanket*, Ben, when confronted with words not known in print, made use of grapho-phonic information but in some instances did so without making adjustments to these readings through his knowledge of syntax and meaning. (For example, *away/always*; *called no/could not.*) Elsewhere, however, he self-corrected—although this was not always crucial (*a/the*). In other instances his miscues were syntactically acceptable, indicated use of grapho-phonic information and made good sense.

Overall, Ben shows active engagement in the task of becoming literate and in making meaning. We note too in his literacy learning (as we would claim in all oral language learning) that he has moved developmentally in a series of approximations which, over time, become more accurate and thus more acceptable as proficient reading and writing. Of course, Ben has been given opportunities to develop in this way both at home and at school.

ENCOURAGING AN INTEGRATED READING AND WRITING PROGRAM

Differences in children's abilities abound and variations in background, needs and learning inclinations occur. However, *even if* such differences mean variation in some children's initial pathway into literacy (Durkin, 1966; Clark, 1976; C. Chomsky, 1971; Y. Goodman, 1980) it makes much sense in schools *to encourage an integrated reading and writing program from the first day of a child's schooling*—as has been done in Ben's case. After all, reading and writing *are* parallel and related processes; they complement and support each other. Undoubtedly, they can be taught together, thus giving each child an opportunity to find his/her particular way into literacy, if that's necessary, and allowing reading and writing to progress in a mutually supportive way.

What might happen, then, if we invite children to write first day of school? Some won't. Some will draw. Some will scribble (but not necessarily to represent writing). Some children will write a collection of idiosyncratic symbols, or actual numbers and letters or odd words. Others will write stories which are constructed using reasonable sound symbol relationships which can be read; some children will write complete words accurately within their stories. This is briefly the probable and natural variation in writing within any group of young children.

The situation with reading is similar. Some children will have little idea. Some will pick up a book and tell a story aloud whilst looking solely at the pictures. Some will recognise accurately many logos within the environment, for example, *Coca Cola* and *McDonalds*. Many children will give functional equivalents for logos. Other children will identify particular important words and letters. Many children will recognise their own name in print. Some children will use the print partially in a story to give an "approximation" of it, and occasionally there will be a child in the group who reads fluently.

As with writing, we invite children, from the beginning of school, to "read" as best they can within a framework of support, encouragement and teaching at the point of need. To do this we require knowledge of *how reading and writing intertwine* as children progress in their literacy development. The following is an attempt to point to some of these relationships.

EARLY SCRIBBLING: CONSTRUCTION OR REPRESENTATION?

Smith (1982a, p. 180) makes an interesting claim that children's early scribbles are constructive rather than representational. That is, the child is primarily concerned with "the creation of something which did not exist in the world before . . . of creating a new world, a possibility which fascinates infants". To the child, this activity is *not writing* in the sense that it represents language and can thus be *said* to mean something. This kind of scribble, which gives no indication of anything else but a construction of a new world and an exploration of the tools in use, would seem not to have a close parallel in reading.

Later (and this is more likely to be so with school age children) scribble becomes representational. The child scribbles beneath his/her drawing or beside it, or indicates, for instance, possible knowledge of spacing through occasional breaks in the line of scribble or written lines of shapes and letters. In each of these we have evidence that the child knows that writing is meant to represent language. To the child, this *is* writing (Smith, 1982a). It's an undertaking with an intention to mean. The child has grasped a crucial concept and demonstrates it.

Parallel development in reading would be behaviour which demonstrates an awareness that meanings can be represented symbolically. The "reading" of the STOP sign, the *Kit Kat* label (even as chocolate) or "talking a story" while turning the pages of a book, shows a realisation that meanings can be represented in a symbolic way. Such "readings" may be done by the child prior to much, if any, specific awareness of the print itself.

Indeed, in response to their own writings, children often invent "messages" without apparent relationship to the written form (Clay, 1975). Or they may ask the adult to read a piece just written, in order to check if the writing has worked. Here the child is wanting to know whether his/her writing is doing what has been hypothesised it should do. When such questions come, and especially questions such as: "How do you write my name?", or the child writes: "A, D, M, A, M, M", then states: "Allison, David, Melanie, Amanda, Mark and Mathew" (Dunstall, 1983, p. 66) then he/she is beginning to move beyond the more general or gross concepts about how print represents language and what the "match" should be when we read such print. Once the child begins to interact with the print on the page when reading, and begins to invent spellings in writing, then clearly attention is being given to the details of our written system.

But let us return to those behaviours such as inventing messages unrelated apparently to the print, and that of the child who, for example, is content to write a letter of the alphabet and read it as a name. The work of Emilia Ferreiro (1978) may help explain, to some extent, such behaviours.

CHILDREN'S CONCEPTUALISATIONS OF WHAT THE WRITTEN WORD REPRESENTS

In a study of four to six year old children, Ferreiro found that: "the written text is not considered as a graphic representation which mirrors the spoken utterance" (p. 38). That is, children, in the early part of their literacy development, do *not* see that a written text is *directly* related to spoken language. It is seen as a system of symbols that has some relationship to writing but not a direct and specific one. Somewhat tentatively, I'd suggest that this conceptualisation by children may help us to understand why a child might seem content with an unrelated "reading" of the printed form or an approximate "reading" of the text (and I might add that such behaviour should not be discouraged but seen as a probable developmental stage). Also, the difficulty some children have in pointing specifically at words in reading, although related to their awareness of what a word is, may be tied also to their conceptualisation that not all words need be represented in graphic

60

form. Ferreiro suggests that young children do not expect the verb to be written, that only the referential (or static) content of the message is represented in the text (p. 38). Later, although the verb is understood to be represented graphically, articles are not. The article "does not comprise enough letters to be 'for reading' " (p. 39).

This is fascinating information. Not only does it help us to understand why children might write certain things, it also helps us to read children's early written language. Let us look at two examples provided by Mehedin and Stuart, both prep. children. Mehedin wrote the following "story":

I got a cat and it's called Squeaky.

When asked to "read" his piece he stated: "I got a cat and it's called Squeaky". At first sight Mehedin's writing appears unrelated to his reading, but if we look at the section after the "full stop" (*Kidtnn Sykn̄t*) it seems feasible that Mehedin has omitted the pronoun and verb and concentrated on the "referential content" (*Kiat Sykn̄t*) but including "and" (*NN*). In his "reading" of his written work he has read a full sentence.

The relationship between Stuart's written text below and his related reading also becomes understandable. His invented spellings demonstrate the way he is relating sound to symbol and Ferreiro's insights explain to us why the articles have been omitted and why he reads his piece as he did.

UKARSHREFLARTEN

You, Mrs Cariss, a tree, a flower, a tent.

SOME IMPLICATIONS FOR TEACHING

This paper then has attempted clarification of certain relationships between writing and reading in the very early years of literacy acquisition, has given a brief account of one child's literacy development from pre-school to Grade I, and has argued that reading and writing learning progresses in a mutually supportive way, i.e. in parallel. Ben's development in literacy supports this view and lends weight to the idea that, within a school program, from prep. grade onwards, *reading and writing should be integrated.*

Why not, on the very first day of school, arrange for writing and reading to arise playfully and authentically without the risk of failure and disappointment (Woods, 1984)? Create a situation or seize an opportunity to have "writing" and "reading" happen—but *real* writing and reading in the sense that the "writing" has an understood purpose for the children's real-life needs, and the reading is of meaningful material that makes sense to children.

In writing, allow children choice. Refrain, as much as possible, from behaviours and language which force attention onto what it might be that the *teacher* wants. Instead, there should be enthusiastic agreement arising from a purposeful and exciting *need* to write. Of course, as mentioned earlier, some children won't write but will draw, some will do little, whilst others will write eagerly. These differences are to be expected and should be tolerated. Some children may not understand, and thus will need time to absorb and to respond later to the relevant demonstrations of reading and writing going on in the room—demonstrations which concentrate on purpose, not form (Smith, 1982b).

As teachers, we must demonstrate constantly authentic writing—a real letter to someone, a list of books to get from the school library, a diary response to a child, a note to the Physical Education teacher, the writing of a story, a rhyme or a recipe. Relevant demonstrations in reading would include the teacher reading *to* children and *with* children and reading silently—reading books, newspapers, notes, labels, ads, lists, instructions, recipes, letters etc.

On the first day, read together a predictable book (e.g. *Mrs Wishy Washy*, Melser & Cowley) or read together rhymes such as *Humpty Dumpty*. These are enjoyable community acts which can suggest powerfully to children that they *can* read. Moreover, such stories and rhymes make sense and are fun. They lend themselves to role play, re-readings and memorisation. Arrange for each child to take home a copy to "read" that night.

As children grow older, those who continue to struggle with the written word, actively constructing their own stories, descriptions etc., develop also their reading proficiency and reading comprehension. Those children who continue to read expand the scope and variety, and improve the fluency, of their writing—and, of course, talking and listening are quite naturally an integral part of this development as well.

REFERENCES

Burningham, J., *The Blanket*, London, Cape, 1979.
Butler, A. and Turbill, J., *Towards a Reading Writing Classroom*, Sydney, P.E.T.A., 1984.
Chomsky, C., "Write First, Read Later", in *Childhood Education*, 47:5, Feb. 1971, pp. 296-299.
Clark, M.M., *Young Fluent Readers*, London, Heinemann, 1976.
Clay, M.M., *What Did I Write?* Auckland, Heinemann, 1975.
Dunstall, J., *The Pre-School Child's Concept of Reading and Knowledge About Written Language*. Unpublished Research Project for Graduate Diploma in Educational Studies: Reading Option, Melbourne, Phillip Institute of Technology, 1983.

Durkin, D., *Children Who Read Early; two longitudinal studies*, New York, Teachers' College Press, 1966.

Dyson, A.H., "Reading, Writing, and Language: Young Children Solving the Written Language Puzzle", in *Language Arts*, 59:8, Nov.-Dec., 1982, pp. 829-839.

Ferreiro, E., "What is Written in a Written Sentence? A Developmental Answer", in *Journal of Education*, 160, Fall 1978, pp. 25-39.

Goodman, Y., "The Roots of Literacy", in *Claremont Reading Conference 44th Yearbook*, edited by M. Douglass. Claremont, CA, Claremont Graduate School, 1980.

Graves, D.H., *Balance the Basics: Let Them Write*, New York, Ford Foundation, 1978.

McDonald, J. and Woodroffe, S.E., *Here is Ben* (basal reading text), Level 2, Book 3, from *Reading 360 Australia*. Melbourne, Cheshire, 1976.

Melser, J. and Cowley, J., *Mrs Wishy Washy*. Melbourne, Rigby Education (Story Box), 1981.

Smith, F., *Writing and the Writer*, London, Heinemann, 1982(a).

Smith, F., "The Creative Achievement of Literacy". Paper presented at University of Victoria Symposium on "Children's Response to a Literate Environment: Literacy Before Schooling", 6-9 Oct., 1982, Canada.

Walshe, R.D., ed., *Donald Graves in Australia—Children Want to Write*, Sydney, P.E.T.A., 1981.

Wilson, L., *Magpies*, Melbourne, Nelson (Country Kids series), 1983.

Woods, C., "Play, Playfulness, Language and Learning", in *Australian Journal of Reading*, 7:2, June 1984, pp. 53-60.

TEACHER ASSISTANCE FOR CHILDREN LEARNING HOW TO LEARN SPELLING

Don Russell
Bouchier Street Primary School
Shepparton (Vic.)

We all recognise what a splendid educational breakthrough the teaching of reading and writing as complementary areas of language has been. When the learner sees that writing and reading are written language companions, he or she comes to recognise that each contributes to the enrichment of the other. By reading one gets the feeling of the form that writing is. By writing one gets the sense of how what one reads is composed. However, regardless of the merits of such a holistic approach for the majority of children who do seem to read, write and spell without systematic, intensive, or structured instruction, it must be recognised that there are some children for whom the method is inadequate. A child hampered by lack of spelling skills will have difficulty in integrating into a mutually supportive developmental process the cognitive and language information available from both the reading and writing act. Lack of spelling skills will lead to inevitable disappointment and feelings of inadequacy, for much of what a child does in school is judged on the basis of written work. It is desirable that decisions made by teachers on behalf of their children should be made on the basis of knowledge about factors related to spelling proficiency and an understanding of the causes of spelling disability. Jorm (1983) holds that spelling disabilities can result from deficits in the basic cognitive processes which underlie the complex spelling skill. If we hypothesise that children internalise information about spoken and written words, organise that information, construct tentative rules based on that information and apply these rules to the spelling of words as part of a language-based activity, it becomes essential that the development of the spelling process is understood by teachers, who must diagnose children's spelling problems and develop effective instructional programs.

STAGES OF SPELLING DEVELOPMENT:

A number of studies (Beers, et al. 1976; Zutell, 1978 and Beers and Beers, 1980) suggest that, as children develop skill in spelling, they move through clearly defined stages which parallel the earlier stages of language development. Spelling proceeds from simple to more complex activities through a reshaping of cognitive structures at each level (Gentry, 1981). For the purpose of this discussion the three stages from research by Beers and Henderson (1977) will be considered.

First Stage

An examination of the invented spellings of beginning spellers indicates that they use letter name strategies and rely heavily on articulatory features to determine the most appropriate letter. At this stage the child is heavily dependent upon the surface structure of language. This points up the importance of oral language as an initial guide to learning to spell. It also indicates that letter sounds should be used for children who are beginning spellers or older spellers having major spelling problems, rather than using both letter names and sounds as part of the instruction, thus requiring the child to work with two coding systems, which may cause unnecessary confusion.

Second Stage

Just as the beginning writer appears to be using orthographic knowledge based on awareness that letters are chiefly symbols for sounds, so children refine their vowel spellings as they seek the letters which represent sounds in the words to be spelt. This stage is usually reached around the middle of Year One when the concept of "word" is firmly established. Here we have the beginnings of meta-linguistic awareness or knowledge of one's own understanding about aspects of language. Unless children have this meta-linguistic awareness they cannot match spoken and written words or come to understand the complex structure underlying a word. Unless children have explicit awareness of how language works, a certain level of meta-linguistic sophistication or level of development, we should not automatically assume that there are linguistic signals directing a child's spelling development. Further, it may be suggested that, for children without meta-linguistic awareness, there can be no system or coherence to a spelling program based solely on a teacher's correction of individual errors found in written work. Generalisations, if any, made on the basis of this limited sample are likely to be incorrect and misapplied.

At this stage in the development of children's spelling skills a deficiency on the automatic or perceptual level of linguistic processing may reflect a lack of meta-linguistic awareness. It is essential, therefore, that instruction is directed towards fostering the link between the tacit knowledge of language with the explicit knowledge of how language works. We should not assume that all children have an understanding of this type of awareness and it will be necessary for teachers to develop activities which will foster meta-linguistic awareness.

Third Stage

At about late Year One or early Year Two, children are generally at a spelling stage between phonetic and correct spelling. They begin to assimilate and apply various funds of information from internalised syntactic rules that control the surface structure of oral language as well as phonetic information. Also at this stage there is an increasing knowledge of the relationships between phonetic, syntactic and morphemic influences on the orthography. The importance of reading skill development in concert with writing and spelling development is essential at this stage. Firth (1980) indicates that, as well as having difficulty in print-to-sound conversion which affects a child's ability to pick up information about spelling, disabled spellers lack full knowledge of orthographic features because they do not use the reading mechanism's "full cues". Whilst a partial processing strategy may be adequate for reading, it is inadequate for writing and spelling.

Many children do not move beyond this transitional stage. Gentry (1981) suggests that for children who have not passed through the phonetic and transitional stages of spelling development, formal spelling instruction will not be of great benefit, but rather will lead to frustration and little success. If it is the case that children are "stuck" in an early stage of spelling developm.ent, then the goal of instruction and the type of activities developed should take into consideration the importance of developing proficiency in language manipulation and understandings prior to the introduction of more formal types of spelling programs. When children have reached a stage of readiness for formal instruction, this should augment rather than replace the child's newly acquired writing habit and considerable time might be spent in hypothesising about the words they want to spell.

COGNITIVE ASPECTS OF SPELLING DEVELOPMENT

Zutell (1979) concluded from his study of children in Years One to Four that for both spelling and cognitive tasks there are significant relationships. He indicated that the development of spelling proficiency involves both cognitive and linguistic processes and, as such, requires the active participation of the learner in a variety of language and cognitive activities. Jorm (1983), in reviewing the cognitive processes used in spelling, indicates that components such as a mental lexicon, sound-to-print correlations and orthographic rules combine into information resources. The learner must apply searching strategies in order to make decisions about the spelling of words. Beginning writers rely heavily on the phonetic, graphemic and orthographic redundancies in language to help them spell. Spelling involves the writer in processing strategies by which the learner utilises language redundancies to reduce the available alternatives. Language needs to be well developed with an extensive base which allows children to make use of phoneme-grapheme correspondences, as well as syntactic and semantic relationships in words which enable children to make predictions in spelling unknown words. In order to help children develop language skills needed for writing and to assist them to understand the writing system, teachers must consciously construct environments in which children are immersed in language and are assisted to develop their spelling skills. Children who have some difficulty in spelling require more assistance in handling the orthography. These children require more opportunities to consciously direct their attention to the general patterns which underly words, and to attend to aspects of morphological relationships among words. Children need to compare and contrast words on a variety of levels—sounds, structure, semantics and syntax—so that they can systematically discover and utilise intraword patterns of organisation.

VISUAL SKILLS

A good speller uses visual associations derived from associative sets of words. From these visual associations children can develop stores of words such as "sight", "right", "might". Other unpredictable words are stored in visual memory as unique items. Visual association and visual representation of unpredictable spellings can be used as a verification channel to check the written form with the visual form in memory. Both of these strategies require the speller to be able to recognise and distinguish individual letters and clusters of letters in words. Indeed, both visual and auditory perception skills are needed by children learning to spell. An awareness of their interrelatedness should encourage perceptual training as an integral part of the total language and spelling development program.

It has been suggested by Beers and Beers (1980) that children will internalise information about words only through repeated experience with words. The experience required includes close visual scrutiny and the capacity to focus attention selectively on relevant stimuli. Bannatyne (1975) suggests several techniques for direct teaching of selective attention. One tactic is to exaggerate the differences between stimuli to be discriminated. Another suggested by Torgesen (1979) and Maker (1981) uses a cognitive modification approach to learning visual discriminations. This technique involves the addition of self-talk, self-reinforcement, and modelling by the teacher, who performs a discrimination task while talking out loud. All of the techniques described here may be very profitably incorporated into protocols which focus on the thinking skills that are brought into play in spelling. A teacher might model the task of deciding which vowel combination is appropriate for a word, thus:

"Now this word *found* that I have to spell. What are the sounds in *found*? *fff-ow-nd*. Yes, *found*. I know the beginning sound, *f*. Now what letters make the *ow* sound? Do I know any other words like *found—sound, round*, etc.? *Ow* has the *ou* sound also—in words like *cow, now*, etc. I will write the word as *fownd* and also *found* and see which one looks better."

The basic premise of this approach is that cognitions (of which inner speech is an aspect) may be modelled by the teacher and emulated by the child. Since the selection of the correct phonemes for written language is a problem-solving process, the steps in the process must be clear to the learner. First, they must be able to get the information required. Second, they must be able to apply cognitive strategies which later become covert guides to the behaviour necessary to spell accurately.

TEACHING APPLICATIONS

Although many children will learn to spell many words informally, direct instruction is needed to help beginning spellers to develop strategies that will enable them to spell unfamiliar words they will need in written communications. This is not to say that correct spelling is over-emphasised—for that can stifle the writing process. Rather, encouragement to spell words children are unsure of, as a means of discovering the phonological and syntactic systems they already know and as a means of fostering hypothesis-testing involvement, is suggested.

Another means of assisting children in the writing process is to assist them in attaining a core vocabulary. There is a consensus in the research that children need to learn a core vocabulary of the essential words for written communication. Such a vocabulary is presented by Thomas (1979) in which he lists the 2000 words most written in today's society. Whilst it is important that children become familiar with the words most often used in writing, it is equally important that the list is supplemented by special words, high interest words, words from context, technical words and community words as well as words presenting particular spelling difficulty.

In some instances it will be necessary for the teacher to examine and present words to be committed to memory. The research findings of Gillet and Kita (1980) show that it is more efficient to present words in lists rather than in context. For some children, it is very important that the word is seen in isolation and thus be better able to concentrate on its visual form. The strategy also enables the application of perceptual clustering techniques so that the essential discriminations may be given due attention. A series of steps which may be used as a teaching strategy or self-study strategy incorporates the following:

1. *See the word in isolation.* Examine the word and its parts. Is there a familiar part? Is there a really tricky part?

2. *Say the word*—with clear enunciation. *Sound the word*—with separation of phonemes.

3. *Write the word*—a number of times and then from memory.

4. *Use the word* in context—and plan to use it as often as possible in the near future.

5. Develop a generalisation link. Does this word fit into a pattern I already know?

In looking at generalisations, there should be a note of caution. It is not intended that rules should be taught in isolation, but rather the emphasis would be on children developing their own generalisations based on working with a variety of words. By considering words such as *piano, solo, banjo, commando, generalissimo* which have a plural "s" ending (as distinct from *tomato* and the "es" plural) it may be seen that the "s" ending is a result of the words being derived from Italian. Through a study of morphemes, root words and interesting derivations (e.g. *rosella* is a corruption of *Rose Hill'ers*—the convict name for the birds seen at Rose Hill) children may be introduced to the rich history of language and its dynamic growth.

CONCLUSION

This paper has reviewed the developmental and cognitive aspects of learning to spell. It suggests that, for many children, teacher intervention will support their acquisition of spelling skills in much the same way as oral language skills were developed—by immersion in a rich language environment, by provision of environmental feed-back on their own developmental patterns and by modelling the cognitive behaviour children need to emulate. As for other language learning, learning to spell requires the active, hypothesis-testing involvement of the learner. In addition, the learner needs to develop strategies that will enable him or her to think objectively about many aspects of language and information-processing strategies that may be brought into play in the progressive formulation of spellings of unknown words. A thorough understanding of the spelling process has implications for teachers as they assist children to learn how to learn spelling.

REFERENCES

Bannatyne, A., "Research Design and Progress in Remediating Learning Difficulties" in *Journal of Learning Disabilities*, 1975, pp. 345-348.

Beers, J.W. and C.S., "Vowel Spelling Strategies First and Second Graders: A Growing Awareness of Written Words" in *Language Arts*, Vol. 57, No. 2, 1980, pp. 166-177.

Beers, J.W. and C.S., and Groat, K., "The Logic Behind Children's Spellings" in *The Elementary School Journal*, Vol. 77, No. 3, 1976, pp. 238-242.

Beers, J.W., and Henderson, E.H., "A Study of Developing Orthographic Concepts among First Graders" in *Research in Teaching English*, Vol. 11, No. 2, 1977, pp. 133-148.

Firth, U., "Unexpected Spelling Problems" in U. Firth (ed.) *Cognitive Processes in Spelling*, London, Academic Press, 1980.

Gentry, R.C., "Learning to Spell Developmentally" in *Reading Teacher*, Vol. 34, No. 4, 1981, pp. 378-381.

Gillet, J., and Kita, J., "Words, Kids and Categories" in Henderson, H., and Beers, J.W., *Developmental and Cognitive Aspects of Learning to Spell*, Newark, International Reading Association, 1980.

Jorgensen, J.K., "What Shall we do with Psychological Processes?" in *Journal of Learning Disabled*, 1979, pp. 514-521.

Jorm, A.F., *The Psychology of Reading and Spelling Difficulties*, London, Routledge and Kegan Paul, 1983.

Maker, C.J., "Problem Solving: A General Approach to Remediation" in Smith, D.D., *Teaching the Learning Disabled*, Englewood Cliffs, Prentice Hall, 1981.

Thomas, V., *Teaching Spelling*, 2nd edn, Chicago, Gage Publishing Co., 1979.

Zutell, J., "Some Psycholinguistic Perspectives on Children's Spellings" in *Language Arts*, Vol. 55, No. 7, 1978, pp. 844-845.

INFANTS' READING BOOKS—STEPPING STONES TOWARDS LITERACY
... But what do they teach?

Peter Freebody and Carolyn D. Baker
University of New England

THE WIDELY-HELD BELIEF

The school books produced for infants depict routine, even banal, events in bland, everyday stories. The words are common, regular and "easy", and the sentences are short and uncomplicated. In summary, the language and the stories are very close to the unremarkable, everyday, conversational world of the child. The rationale for this is that infants' readers are intended almost solely to teach infants how to read in the most elementary sense of the term "read"—that is, how to decode the graphic script into oral language. The books are not meant primarily to impart content.

THE LIKELY TRUTH

Recently a number of researchers have pointed to some differences between written and spoken language which place distinct demands on the reader *over and above* the obvious needs to decode the graphic symbols (e.g. Rubin, 1980; Olson, 1977). In particular, Olson has drawn attention to how forms used in written language serve to embody and shape particular forms of knowing and communicating. In fact, Olson regarded the process of induction to these literate forms of knowing and communicating as *so central to the educational enterprise* that he concluded that "schooling is a matter of mediating the relationship between children and the printed text" (Olson, 1977, p. 66).

Since infants' first school books are important objects in the infants' transition from being pre-literate to being literate, they necessarily introduce preceptual, intellectual, and social-communicational techniques. Some of these techniques operate in very obvious ways and some are more subtle. Obviously, children's first school readers are intended to help in early decoding instruction; more subtly, they are stepping-stones from *everyday, conversational* ways of communicating and thinking toward those forms of communicating and thinking which apply in a *written, literate* context. The infants' readers have important linguistic and cultural roles which literate adults, who take for granted the particular linguistic and cultural forms involved, simply may not "see".

A powerful way of introducing the linguistic and cultural forms used in literate culture to children is to (apparently) depict **the familar culture** of the children—with themselves at the centre, surrounded by family, friends, and the home and school environments—but to depict this culture in **the special language** of the *literate* culture. Thus, the everyday, conversational experiences and utterances of the children are moulded into ways of expressing, interacting, and knowing which characterise the culture offered *by the school.* The children's world *seems* to be reflected back to them in the books but, in fact, the children are being shown their own world through the eyes of the *literate culture.*

Thus the infants' first school books are largely about the infants themselves: they inform children of a particular concept of "childhood" and, especially, of "school-childhood" and "literate-childhood". The authority of the school, endorsed by parents and the larger society, transmits its versions of these important concepts to children, in their earliest encounters with the school, in part through the books. Books are highly valued objects—almost objects of reverence—and these "holy" writings appear to describe the world of their readers. Examination of the details of how this depicted world is different from the actual, out-of-school, conversational world of the children reveals some of the fine mechanisms of formal induction into literacy.

THE EVIDENCE

The authors of this article have recently been engaged in an extensive study of the language used in a wide range of readers produced for infants' grades in Australia. Included in the surveyed infants' readers were those commonly used in a representative educational division of New South Wales. This division contained 65 classes of children in their first and second years of schooling. Also included were readers pub-lished recently by the major relevant publishing houses in

Australia. A total of 163 basal and supplementary readers comprised the corpus of language. There were 83,819 words of running text in these readers, and 2474 different words. The interested reader is referred to Gay and Freebody (1984) for the complete word list.

We conducted our analyses under a number of headings. We examined first the *most common words* in the corpus; we asked *"Who populates* the readers?", itemising and discussing the human and non-human characters who frequently appear; the issue of differences in *usage* between *male* and *female* descriptors was addressed; and, finally, we noted some of the ways in which *conversations* between adults and children in the infants' readers contrast with everyday, oral (i.e. real) conversations. In this article we briefly summarise some of our findings.

Initially we simply examined the most common words in the infants' readers. The twenty most common words account for 34.4% of *all* the text in *all* of the 163 infants' books. In order of frequency these are: *the, and, a, to, I, said, is, you, in, he, it, can, they, me, here, on, says, little, go,* and *for.* We compared the most frequent words in the infants' readers with those from the language spoken by five-and-a-half year old children (Hart, 1974).

A couple of points of contrast can be noted. In the readers, the word *the* is by far the most common word, accounting on average for about one word in 14 throughout the whole text. In oral language, however, *the* is ranked only fifth, accounting only for about one word in 50. In written language, longer discourses on a single topic are expected than in spoken language, which occurs in episodically more fragmented contexts. That is, in oral language, objects and people would be expected to come and go in more rapid and varied succession than in written language. The exception is, of course, the speaker himself or herself, who remains a constant reference point in everyday, spoken interaction, as reflected in the most frequent word spoken—*I.* This in turn accounts for the relatively lighter duty performed by *the* when speaking, since *the* generally signals co-reference with, or at least entailment in, a word previously introduced. This reflects simply the fact that the speaker uses language as an integral operator in, and commentator on, daily life, while the writer is engaged in the production of an *artifice,* one of the key attributes of which is the pursuit of a theme, where people and objects are traced through time. So, in this fundamental respect, literate use of language can be seen as a different type of activity in the world from the conversational use of language.

One way in which the infants' readers offer the child a transition point between the everyday and the literate uses of language is reflected in the extremely frequent use of the word *said* in the infants' books. If we combine the frequencies of *said, say* and *says,* we find that the "say family" fills second place on the word list behind *the.* This indicates the extraordinary prevalence of the reportage of talk in the infants' readers. These books are crammed with dialogue, reported directly, and not reported second-hand by the narrator. Thus the text calls explicitly and continually on the oral tradition of the child. However, this similarity to actual oral language and conversation is, in some respects, misleading. There are important differences between actual, everyday conversations which children may be involved in and the ways conversations are portrayed in these readers. For example, in the infants' readers we find that conversations are reported in these forms:

(a) "Verbatim talk of speaker," said speaker. "More verbatim talk of speaker." (This form accounts for about 55% of represented talk.)
and
(b) "Verbatim talk of speaker," said speaker. (This form is used about 40% of the time.)

The form which most directly and unambiguously indicates the speaker's identity is the dramatist's form of naming the speaker first and then showing the talk. This technique is used only about 5% of the time. At first sight it would seem that recognition of speaker change and current speaker identification would be made easier if "speaker said" or even merely "speaker:" were placed before the verbatim talk. Shifts between speakers are quite obvious in oral conversations and are crucial to an understanding of the differences between characters in a story, and hence of the plot itself.

What is the force of representing conversation in the above ways? We suggest that the placement of the narrator's "speaker said" contributions makes the reader dependent on the occasional input of the narrator. Room is made for the narrator in the discourse. The narrator's voice both contextualises and announces which speakers say what. We see this as a step toward the more fully narrator-controlled presentation of talk in which the actual words spoken are subsumed under the interpretive "authority" of the narrator's voice (e.g. "Jack tried hard to open the box, but he complained . . ."). In this unobtrusive way, children are introduced to the persona of narrator, a vital interpretive presence in text which will come to assume more and more centrality in their dealings with the written word.

In addition, oral language occurs in a *flow* which is broken by pauses for breath, which contains cadences and other rhythmic qualities, stumbling, vocalisations, interruptions, backtracking, and repetition of words, and which does not happen in upper and lower case letters or in clusters which approximate grammatical units. The oral language represented in the infants' books is broken by "speaker said" at points separating sentences and clauses, not necessarily where speakers might themselves pause. Segmenting language in these ways displays to the child the literate culture's notions of sentence, clause and phrase. Speakers are *made* to talk in sentences, clauses and phrases. Child-characters who speak in the texts are portrayed as literate, in that their speech is made to adhere to the grammatical rules they will later learn through written forms.

If these books are thought of as important aspects of a transition toward literate school life, then not only are the above structural/linguistic aspects of the written word significant, but so also are the content of the stories and the regularities underlying them. For example, in our analyses we observed some blatant and not-so-blatant instances of *male-centred* language and content. A blatant example is the substantial frequency advantage enjoyed by the group *boy/boys/man/men* over the group *girl/girls/woman/women*. There are significantly more males, young and old, than females in the infants' books. At a less obvious level, we found that *boy* is statistically more likely to occur than *boys*, but that *girl* and *girls* are equally likely to appear. That is, boys are more likely to appear as individuals—girls are not. Similarly, the most frequently applied adjective in the infants' readers, *little*, is applied to girl/s more frequently than it is to boy/s. Perhaps in these ways the implicit, officially-sanctioned views of the broader society are conveyed to infants—or at least reinforced.

TEMPORARY CONCLUSIONS

We have pursued the notion that infants' readers are designed not only to help teach the perceptual skills of reading but also to introduce some of the peculiar ways language is used in literate contexts. We have attempted to outline parts of the "world" described in the readers, and to detail some aspects of this peculiar language use. In this summary we have mentioned differences in the pattern of highly frequent words in written and spoken contexts, the prevalence of dialogue and the differences between the portrayal of dialogue in the books and its actual characteristics, and some instances of male-centredness.

One of the major functions of research into the differences between spoken and written language is to delineate the directions in which we might expand our conceptions of how children are inducted into the forms of literacy. We have suggested some directions this expansion might take. If an instructor is unaware of a particular significant dimension of the material to be learned, then he or she will draw attention to that dimension, if at all, in only indirect or inconsistent ways. In that case, at best, the infant can expect a patchy and covert treatment of certain important (and, incidentally, very interesting) aspects of the problem of becoming a literate school child.

N.B. *A more complete analysis and discussion of our research can be found in Freebody and Baker (1984), Freebody and Gay (1984), and Gay and Freebody (1984).*

REFERENCES

Freebody, P. and Baker, C.D. *Children's First School Books; Introductions to the culture of literacy.* Unpublished paper, University of New England, 1984.

Freebody, P. and Gay, J. *Statistical and Semantic Analyses of the Words in Infants' Readers.* Unpublished paper, University of New England, 1984.

Gay, J. and Freebody, P. *An Australian Basic Word List for Beginning Reading.* Unpublished paper, University of New England, 1984.

Olson, D.A. "The Language of Instruction; the literate bias of schooling" in R.C. Anderson, R.J. Spiro and W.E. Montague (eds), *Schooling and the Acquisition of Knowledge.* Hillsdale, N.J., Lawrence Erlbaum, 1977.

Rubin, A.A. "A Theoretical Taxonomy of the Differences Between Oral and Written Language" in R.J. Spiro, B.C. Bruce and W.F. Brewer (eds), *Theoretical Issues in Reading Comprehension.* Hillsdale, N.J., Lawrence Erlbaum, 1980.

TEACHING WRITING

Attend to "Skills" as Part of "Process"

R.D. Walshe
Author of **Better Reading/Writing—Now** *and*
Every Child Can Write *(P.E.T.A.)*

> *If we think of writing primarily as a skill, we tend to concentrate upon errors . . . [But if] we think of writing as a form of behaviour, we tend to direct attention to the psychology of the total act from beginning to end, including the errors. Writing is not the words on paper alone. Writing is overcoming inhibitions . . . getting started . . . controlling . . . matching words to thoughts . . . feeling as well as thinking.*—**William F. Irmscher**, *College English*, December 1977.

Modern research into "the process of writing" gives us a much clearer picture of how real writers write than we have ever had before. As a result, many teachers are trying out new ways of conducting the class's "Writing Time" in a bid to allow students to experience "the real process" instead of drudging mechanically through writing exercises.

But is this new process-aware approach attentive to "skills"? Won't the focus on process divert students from the "correctness" that society demands of writing? These questions come from conscientious teachers who fear that anything less than a main emphasis on "skills" will open the classroom door to sloppy expression.

First, however, we must ask: Which skills? The skills these teachers have in mind are chiefly those which have long been the concern of the school's traditional writing exercise (the "composition"), namely spelling, punctuation, grammar and usage. They are also the only writing skills spoken of in society at large, which sees writing as a mechanical matter of applying these "skills" to "what one wants to say".

But the new "process" research shows that spelling, punctuation, grammar and usage are only *some* of the elements that enter into a writing task. We term them collectively the *conven-*

tions *of writing*, or the *surface features of writing*, because they are the elements visible to the reader. The skills needed to get them right are properly limited by the term "surface skills".

Real (as opposed to exercise) writing demands more of a writer than a control of the surface skills. It demands skills of perceiving a real experience or problem, of collecting ideas, of defining the subject, of conceiving an approach, of establishing a tone, of getting started, of working intently at thinking-drafting-revising . . . and much else. In short, manifold skills are required for what is above all a *process of meaning-making*.

This meaning-making is the writer's *basic* responsibility, while the surface correctness is a *secondary*, though nonetheless important, responsibility.

Yet the traditional approach termed the surface skills "the basics of writing". It was a misconception that gave rise to generations of dull composition writing backed by even duller drilling of the surface skills. No wonder only a small minority of students emerged from the schools with positive feelings about writing. The rest had decided: "I can't write. I hate writing. I'll avoid it whenever I can."

So the considered answer of anyone who understands writing as the complex process it is, will go like this: "I am as concerned as anyone to help students become proficient in the surface skills, BUT I know there's a better way to teach them than the drills-and-composition routine. The striving for correctness needs to take place *within*—as part of—the process of meaning-making. Moreover, it needs to be carried out as much as possible by the writer, not the teacher, as self-correction, though the teacher will of course be close by, ready to help. In particular, the teacher will encourage self-correction at the revision stage, after the first draft has concentrated on getting the meaning into some shape. So, while elevating writing as a process of meaning-making, I will certainly be attending to the 'correctness' skills, and can do so now in a classroom which no longer turns students away from writing."

HOW TEACHABLE IS WRITING?

You can't teach anyone to write, but you can teach them a lot about writing.—**Anon.**

One's native language is always more learned than taught. Linguists know this well. They point to the "miracle" of young children "learning to talk by talking" without the benefit of adult teaching—no "skills of speech" or "skills of grammar", and only slight correction of vocabulary and usage.

So too is it possible to "learn to write by writing", though not

without great effort. Individuals have managed it untaught, but children fortunately have a dozen school years to learn with the help of teachers.

The first responsibility of good teaching is to get real writing started, the students writing keenly on topics that interest them, topics that are as much as possible self-chosen. This looks after the main *learning* factor, the involving of each child in "learning to write by writing" (along with reading). Then the teacher can intervene judiciously at any point in the process with suggestions for improving particular skills, and do so in some confidence that the suggestions—these being the main *teaching* factor—will be learnt because they offer not skills-in-general but the specific skills needed right now by a particular learner.

The right order is: get willing "process writing" under way, then cultivate self-correction as part of the process and assist where individual need becomes apparent.

To make this clear, however, is only the beginning of showing the advantages of a "process of writing" approach over a "skills of writing" approach. The "process" teacher finds it possible to take a far more comprehensive view of writing teaching, and will typically try to . . .

1. *Provide an environment which fosters writing:* plenty of time to write daily, an abundance of reading material, daily reading aloud ("the sound of words on paper"), classmates interested in reading and able to comment on one another's

writing, and a teacher who shows enthusiasm for writing by sometimes writing with the class to model and share the craft.

2. *Provide regular opportunities to experience the full process of writing:* while some writing unavoidably remains at first-draft stage, opportunities for "publication" are a recurring incentive to engage in a full process of drafting-revising-publishing, including the self-correction that gets the conventions right.

3. *Provide attention to specific skills:* through (i) individual "conference", as the teacher talks with each student on one or more occasions during the student's process; (ii) group "conference", as the teacher talks with several students who have a skill problem in common; (iii) occasional whole-class demonstration, or revision, or drill of a widely needed skill.

4. *Provide attention to a broader range of "teachables of writing" than spelling, punctuation, usage and grammar:* attention, for example, to PROCESS, by often considering the sequence of thoughts and acts by which each piece of writing develops; REGISTER, the appropriate adjustment of writing to the specific needs of each task (specific subject, form, mood, readership); and MODELS, not only good passages from literature or from student or teacher writing, but also writers' accounts of their craft—their techniques and their even more important efforts to open their eyes and their imaginations to the world around them and within.

"PROCESS" AND "SKILLS" OF A 5 YEAR OLD

Children are intuitive grammarians. If they were not, they would be unable to reach the state of language knowledge evidenced on entrance to school. Our attitudes towards children's use of language . . . can either help or hinder further development of language knowledge.—**Paula Menyuk,** in *"Discovering Language with Children"* (NCTE, 1980)

The healthy interaction of *learning* with *teaching*—of the student's whole-process writing ("learning to write by writing") with the teacher's interventions to cultivate specific skills (attention to "teachables")—can be observed most clearly in relation to beginners, before the onset of the full complexity of writing. When 5 year old Helen wrote

81

her kindergarten teacher at Grays Point Public School (N.S.W.) saw she had written a perfectly grammatical English sentence, "The wind is blowing at me".

The sentence was the result of a *process of writing* fostered by the teacher: the children had discussed and drawn pictures of their windy playground; Helen had further collected ideas by talking with a friend; next day she had thoughtfully worked at her writing; and having read it several times she had edited "my" to "mi".

The teacher perceived that Helen had used many skills in the writing: skills of handwriting, spelling, word-choice, grammar, and the rudimentary punctuation of left-to-right direction and separation of words, not to mention semantic skills of meaning and imagination. Even "style" had been achieved in communicating the charming egocentrism of a purposeful wind blowing at important ME.

This 5 year old is already writing originally and learning intently in *all* the areas of "writing skills". She is mainly "learning to write by writing", not by separate skill-drills. How should her teacher respond to Helen's first school "story"? How develop Helen's "skills" by teaching?

Should she, for instance, list 10 (or 50?) further skills and drill-and-test them day by day in whole-class conditions? She knew that would blight Helen's enthusiasm for writing, perhaps irreparably. Instead she searched out Helen's *individual* need. She glowed with pleasure: "It's a lovely story, Helen!" Then: "Is there anything you want me to help with?" Helen pointed: *mi* doesn't look right. "Oh, but it's a good guess," said the teacher and sounded *m-e*, letting Helen write it in.

This beginning writer was left feeling good about writing and she had eagerly learnt the "skill" of spelling *me* correctly. But what about the other things that might have been "corrected": the *d* that should have been *b*, the spelling of *blowing*, and the absence of a capital and full-stop? At this stage her teacher judged these could wait. Experience told her that small children usually take in only one "teaching point" at a single conference. Moreover, *d*s and *b*s were to come up in tomorrow's handwriting session; Helen would soon get *blowing* right by her own efforts; and capitals and full-stops would get plenty of emphasis in coming weeks. Anyway, Helen's classmates would raise some of these points with her when they read her work. Helen is *learning* fast—from her writing, her reading, her teacher's suggestions, and her classmates' comments.

[If Helen's piece had been intended for "publication", it would have been finally edited by the teacher, after an explanation that editing for publication is the rule throughout society, because readers expect to receive the standard written form of the language.]

AFTERWORD
Writing Is Always "A Wholly New Start"
If learning the "skills of writing" could solve the writing problem, then any writer in command of those skills would enact writing effortlessly. But even professionals can't do that. T.S. Eliot, no less, spoke of the "intolerable wrestle with words and meanings". He knew all the tricks of the trade, all the surface skills, yet twenty years' experience did not save him from the recurring "wrestle" for meaning:

> Trying to learn to use words, and every attempt
> Is a wholly new start, and a different kind of failure
> Because one has only learnt to get the better of words
> For the thing one no longer has to say, or the way in which
> One is no longer disposed to say it. And so each venture
> Is a new beginning, a raid on the inarticulate . . .
>   ("East Coker", The Four Quartets)

. . . every attempt is a wholly new start . . ."

WRITING PROCESS HAS GROWING PAINS

Donald Graves
Director, Writing Process Laboratory
University of New Hampshire

Writing process work has spread like wildfire in North America, Australia and New Zealand. Implementation has been so rapid that teachers and school systems are going through some natural growing pains. These growing pains offer us new opportunities to grow and share in the excitement of children learning. Growing pains often show themselves in **orthodoxies** or short cuts *that bypass listening to children.* We need to identify some of the orthodoxies that have crept into our work. Orthodoxies sound like this: "Make sure he revises at least three times," or "He should publish at least two more times before the year is out," or "Do you use the four- or seven-step approach to the writing process?" Notice the emphasis on numbers. These are dangerous statements *because they bypass the child.* The professionals who make these statements can't listen to children because of poor preparation for process work, or their personal teaching/learning stance is one of inflexibility rather than growth and exploration.

TOO RAPID EXPANSION

Teachers have good reasons for relying on orthodoxies, numbers or methodologies. They are often asked to take on process work after only a single two-hour workshop. Worse, they have never seen professionals demonstrate the writing process with children. If we advocate that children see teachers write, and that modelling is important, then those who prepare teachers must model what they advocate in writing process *by actually demonstrating with children.* Just as surgeons model in the amphitheatre, or barristers handle test cases in the courtroom, we must show what we mean by demonstrating in our laboratory, the classroom. I now accept no workshop engagements with teachers unless the local school system will provide a classroom where I can demonstrate with children.

The heart of writing process work is listening to children. Because listening often requires a philosophical shift and much teacher preparation, most of the orthodoxies become maxims that bypass the listening step. Listening is also hard work for teachers because they find that school materials or curriculum guides are not based on evidence supplied from the children themselves. In child development classes, or in diagnostic programs, professionals hear: "First observe and listen to the child, then act". But teachers find that school materials and curriculum guides are not based on listening to children. Teachers find listening is even more difficult when administrators do not listen to them. Listening is not just something that occurs between teacher and child—it must be the essential communication mode for everyone.

We need to do a reappraisal of growing pains associated with the astonishing growth of writing process practice around the world. In this article I will examine backgrounds essential to continuing teacher growth in the writing process, as well as the orthodoxies surrounding problems in listening to children. There are some practices that deal with both issues—teacher learning and process orthodoxies—that I think will help us to continue to learn from the children.

TEACHER BACKGROUND AND LEARNING STANCE

After ten years of working with writing process, several traits emerge as essential for effective work with children and writing. What I list here are traits that apply to all teaching, not just the teaching of writing. They are obvious, but they cannot be bypassed before looking at ways of dealing with orthodoxies and the teacher's listening to children. The ultimate success of writing process is dependent on the teacher's own learning, reading and writing, and ability to organise a classroom for listening to children.

TEACHER LEARNING: Teachers have to be actively engaged in learning themselves and the children have to see and know it. They share their reading and writing with children and discuss the edges of their learning. These teachers have learned *to trust themselves as learners*. They know their own learning voice and often sound like this in the classroom:

"I was reading the other day that . . ."

"What do you think of the way I've written this?"

"Now I hadn't thought of that, Aleka. That's a good idea. What do you think you will do with it?"

"I don't know the answer to that one. I think I'll check to find out. Where do you think I might check first?"

Teachers who make these statements speak about learning as discovery, as a co-operative activity, and they are pleased when they encounter an opportunity for personal learning or for the children in their classroom.

TEACHERS SHARE THEIR OWN WRITING AND READING: The teachers are aware of a personal and continued involvement in writing and reading. They continue to learn about writing and reading because they practise it and share it with others. I find that more and more teachers come together in afternoons or evenings to share their own excitement with learning or literacy. Right now I am conducting research with Prof. Jane Hansen on how teachers and administrators change their approach to reading and writing through their own regular weekly meetings away from school. The atmosphere at such meetings is relaxed: coffee, tea or soft drinks are served while teachers share what they actually read and write and then help each other to bring their creations to fruition. Many have now published. They learn to listen to each other. Isolated teachers depend on orthodoxies because they don't have a chance to test observations of their children on colleagues.

These same teachers, because they share what they read and write, visit each other's classrooms, observe conferences, and help each other teach. In this building circulation increases, isolation decreases, and orthodoxies wane when teachers can talk about their own reading and writing as well as the children they teach.

Teachers learn about writing through sharing their efforts.

ORGANISATION: The writing conference is the meeting place for listening to children tell about what they know and how they know it. If teachers are to listen to children they must be organised. That is, their children have to know precisely how the room functions, how they accept responsibility and solve problems by themselves. This, in turn, establishes a climate in which children can learn to listen to each other. Teachers have to know how to delegate responsibility and run a highly predictable classroom if they are to ask the challenging, unpredictable questions essential to the writing conference. Teachers who are not organised tend to rely on maxims or orthodoxies to deal with chaos. But, part of being organised is *understanding the process of what is being taught, namely writing.*

WRITING ORTHODOXIES

Orthodoxies usually get expressed as absolutes. In fact, this is one of the best ways to spot an orthodoxy. The use of numbers, absolutes (never, always) or directions given without child evidence are helpful indicators to both listener and speaker that an orthodoxy has taken over. The following are four of the orthodoxies I hear and read most frequently. They are composites of many statements and are expressed in extreme form:

1. Children ought to revise everything they compose.
2. Children should only write in personal narrative: imaginative writing ought to be discouraged.
3. Children should have several conferences for each piece of writing.
4. Spelling, grammar, and punctuation are unimportant.

The rest of this article will discuss these orthodoxies and make recommendations to deal with the problems inherent in each. The overall success a teacher has in dealing with these issues rests in the teacher's own broad-based stance toward learning and classroom organisation.

REVISION: "Children ought to revise everything they compose."

The most common orthodoxy is revision. The teacher holds that no writing is worth its salt unless it has been revised. This is a reaction to the old approach in writing where little was revised. To a large degree revision should occur because the child sees information he would like to change in the piece. The child cares about the topic and wants to change it.

Most pieces are *not revised.* There are not that many pieces that are "hot" or going somewhere. Most of children's writing is intended to just get information on paper.

Writing is also revised when the child and teacher sense the need to go toward final copy, or when work will be read by broader audiences. In this instance the publishing step brings in more refinements with information and surface conventions.

Very young children (aged five, six and seven) often revise by writing four or five pieces on the same subject. They are not consciously revising but their pieces continue to grow as information is refined from one piece to another.

IMAGINATIVE WRITING: "Children should only write in personal narrative. Imaginative writing ought to be discouraged."

This orthodoxy requires children to write only personal narrative. Fiction is outlawed. I have said that it is important for children to write about what they know, but what some children know can best be expressed in *fiction.*

Unfortunately, some children do not have exposure to good fiction or a rich diet of children's literature. If there is little sharing of literature, then children revert to regurgitating last night's television plots. Fiction does not become a means of personal discovery—it is only the manipulation of another person's plots.

CONFERENCES: "Children should have several conferences for each piece of writing."

Conferences are difficult because so much is required to effectively listen to children. All three of the Teacher Background/Learning statements discussed earlier prepare us for listening to children. A few more guidelines are needed to help teachers with conferences.

The most typical orthodoxy about conferences is: "You have to have a conference with each child and on every step of the process". The same teacher returns in a week and says: "It can't be done. Process isn't for me or the children". Under those circumstances the teacher is right. Soon the teacher says: "Conferences take too long. I can't spend ten minutes with each child's piece, and at every step of the writing process". This teacher is correct. No child should receive such extensive attention. That amount of attention usually means the teacher is taking too much responsibility for the child's piece.

The average conference length is about 90 seconds. In that 90 seconds I want the child to speak first about several things: "This is what my piece is about; this is where I am in the draft, and this is what I will do next or what I want help with next". At first, I conduct conferences by circulating around the room; I am not yet ready to have children come to me in one location. By moving around the room I am in closer touch with what is actually happening. Besides, the children are usually assured by my presence that help is not far away.

The help I give is more in the form of receiving the child's work and then asking questions: "Ah, I see you are writing about your swimming team; how does your coach help you to train? Do you have a scheduled training program?" It is much better to have short and frequent contact with children than lengthy discussions. In this way, control of the process stays with the child, and teacher talk is at a minimum.

Most teachers slide into lengthy, impossible conferences because they are trying to teach too much, a very common problem when first starting out. They try to "correct" all writing problems with each piece and in one conference. Teachers can count on other children learning by over-hearing what you do as you travel around the room.

Review the folders in the classroom to see who really needs your help the night before conducting conferences. Some children may need you for two very short conferences, especially if they are struggling writers. Other writers may only need to see you every three or four days.

CONVENTIONS: "Spelling, grammar, and punctuation are unimportant."

I think many educators would like to believe process work is unconcerned with these very important tools. To some degree I am sympathetic with those professionals who believe that process persons have neglected them. In some instances they are right. Some work that children have called good, final copy is needlessly sloppy.

Grammar, punctuation and spelling are important when a child is taking a piece to final copy, when the information is rich and the writer is obviously involved in the piece. In earlier drafts, or in quick drafts, I am more interested in content, in helping the writer to deepen the information. But some pieces are just quick recordings—"thinking aloud", so to speak. With each piece I try to teach one or two new tools to help the child acquire a gradual accumulation of skills. In the course of a year, a child should acquire many new skills because both teacher and child can see how skills enhance meaning.

Finally, much of the work on conventions and proof-reading should be done by the child. I want children to do a personal audit. I want them to circle words they think are misspelled, put boxes around locations where they think punctuation may be needed, or ovals where there might be the need for capitals, or apostrophes. When children do the audit first, then I can see what to teach.

These conventions are essential to clear writing. Teaching them, and insisting on what is possible for the child, is an important expectation, but must come at the right time. When a

child is still struggling with the meaning and content of his piece, stressing the right word, spelling or punctuation is premature teaching and a waste of child and teacher time. Conventions are usually in poor shape when the child starts to discover his subject. Sentences are vague, convoluted, and filled with assumptions. When teachers help the writer to clarify the subject, they are also helping the child to prepare later for more effective use of conventions. When the information is clear, the child can better tell where one idea ends and the other begins. Full stops can then be more accurately placed between two ideas.

A FINAL REFLECTION

Teachers need help, not criticism, in working with the writing process. There has been a kind of bandwagon effect that has forced many teachers into process work without proper preparation. Others have jumped in enthusiastically, eager to see what children can do. And the children haven't disappointed us. Early returns on process work have been exciting. Teachers have been amazed to find that children want to write. But after that first burst of enthusiasm, and large collections of children's work, the orthodoxies appear. People start to come up with maxims or orthodoxies that bypass listening to the child.

We can spot orthodoxies, the lack of listening to children if we listen to our own words and the words of our friends. We use numbers, and absolute words like *always* and *never*, and above all we cease to tell fresh stories about the children we have worked with today.

We need to help each other, as professionals, both through in-service and continued contact with each other. In an era of tight budgets and little money for in-service education, teachers and administrators can set out on their own to help each other. They can meet to share their own writing and reading. More and more teachers are finding such approaches are not just another meeting but are actually life-giving. They meet regularly for an hour away from school. Such contact opens up sharing outside of the building and subsequently within the building.

Teachers who talk outside of school, talk inside school. They visit one another's classrooms, and show how they confer with children during writing. They also send children experienced with conferences to help other children in rooms where teachers are new to writing process. When a child makes a breakthrough on a piece, he not only reads it to his own class, but is sent to share with other classes as well. Statements about orthodoxies are replaced by stories of child victories. Such stories give energy to teachers as well as increase bonds among the professional community.

This article first appeared in *Primary Education*, Vol. 15, No. 4, 1984, and is reprinted here by kind permission of Dove Publications.

LEARNING AT ITS BEST
And Thinking and Writing Too
R.D. Walshe
Author of **Better Reading/Writing—Now** *and*
Every Child Can Write *(P.E.T.A.)*

Is learning at its best in your classroom?

Amid well-conceived projects, a good deal of school practice still tends to treat the student as "empty vessel" or "sponge", passively absorbing information from imposed reading, listening, copying and rather mechanical exercises.

Yet most teachers have long agreed with the view that the best learning is "discovery learning", the kind that calls for inquiry or problem-solving by an active learner.

How can that active—perceptive, creative, critical—learning be expanded?

Of course, learning depends on many factors: the general predisposing *conditions* of home and classroom, and the specific *procedures* for handling what the curriculum requires.

This article is about the procedures. It takes for granted reasonable classroom conditions, including a friendly and helpful teacher.

LEARNING HOW TO LEARN

Can we agree that schooling, on its intellectual side, succeeds only to the extent that a student "learns how to learn"? And that each year should contribute something to making the student a fairly independent learner by Year 12?

Not surprisingly, support for this view has grown swiftly in the recent decades of "knowledge explosion". No one can keep up with the accelerating discoveries of content ("facts") in even one subject, let alone several, but learners can be taught the broad structure and characteristic procedures of the subjects they study so that they know how to go about solving problems within those subjects. This is learning-how-to-learn.

It explains the current curriculum emphasis on cultivating *thinking skills*—or, more specifically, *learning skills*. There is

92

even some agitation for "separate teaching of thinking skills", that is, for a new subject to be added to our crowded curriculum.

But separate teaching of "thinking skills" can be an artificial exercise which achieves little transfer of such skills to real life problems. Better, surely, to integrate careful thinking with each day's real problems: the schools, in all their learning activities, should be consciously working on "the development of generalised ways of attacking problems and on knowledge which can be applied to a wide range of new situations", as Benjamin S. Bloom remarked long ago in his famous *Taxonomy of Educational Objectives*.

He brings us back to the need for more "discovery learning". But what exactly is it, and what forms might it take?

LEARNING AT ITS BEST

Rebelling against the passive "sponge" or "empty vessel" images of learning, we should be looking to the great thinking-models of western culture which underlie discoveries in the arts, the sciences, the technologies. They are what we term the "creative process", the "scientific process", and the "problem-solving process". The chart on page 95 presents recognised sequences of these processes.

By lining up the "stages" of the processes the chart establishes that all of them share *a common sequence* of thought and action. It shows too that writing, which has only recently been understood as a *process*, also shares that sequence.

This common sequence provides educators with the master key to our culture's thinking-at-its-best.

The chart concludes that all four processes are forms or variations of what is necessarily a "learning process". There are some other modes of learning, as the chart observes, but the four lay special claim to teachers' attention because they identify the main ground of learning-at-its-best.

How much of this kind of learning goes on each day in your classroom?

THE IMPORTANCE OF WRITING IN LEARNING

The chart throws into sharp relief the importance of writing as a mode of thinking and learning. In doing so it exposes the shallowness of our society's usual relegation of writing to "service functions" such as recording, communicating and testing.

Clearly, writing can be a significant *means of learning*, that is, of discovering knowledge, getting to know it thoroughly, and using it intelligently. This is good news in every subject area. The teacher who succeeds in lifting the level of the students' writing is in fact lifting overall learning performance to the extent that writing is used across most subjects.

93

If this assessment seems to emphasise the importance of writing at the expense of other channels of learning, I would add at once that the other three language modes (reading, listening, talking) can, and usually should, enter usefully into the process of learning. But more often than not it will be writing that most carefully relates the ideas gathered from all sources, "objectifying" them on the page where they can be revised to produce the deepest understanding (learning) a student can achieve. In short, writing can be a deeper kind of thinking than is otherwise possible.

THE MAJOR AND MINOR USES OF WRITING-TO-LEARN

The chart enables us to deduce one major and at least six minor uses of writing as a means of learning in any subject area.

The MAJOR use is its employment as a "full process of writing" to work out a problem (e.g. a Year 6 research report which answers the question, "Are spiders nothing more than dangerous pests?" or "Why is the consumption of fast foods rising despite warnings about their low quality?").

The MINOR uses are any of the many forms of writing which can be specific to any "stage" of a learning process. Here are examples:

PROBLEM ... write to formulate a problem exactly.

INVESTIGATION ... make notes of ideas, observations, research.

INSIGHT ... capture in writing an inspiration, pattern, lead.

DRAFTING ... brainstorm and/or plan, then produce a rough draft.

POLISHING ... clarify a draft by revising, improving, re-writing.

ANNOUNCEMENT ... write a polished piece of writing which reports effectively, as essay, article, letter etc.

SUMMARY
The Importance of Writing as a Mode of Learning

The great thinking-models underlying progress in the arts, sciences and technologies are the "creative process", "scientific process" and "problem-solving process".

Comparison [see the chart] reveals that they share a common sequence of thought and action; and the more recently understood "writing process" shares this sequence too. All four are necessarily variations of a powerful *learning process*.

Thus the significance of writing as a means of learning is dramatically exhibited, and the teacher who wishes to promote

LEARNING AT ITS BEST

	PROBLEM	INVESTIGATION	INSIGHT	DRAFTING	POLISHING	ANNOUNCEMENT	REACTION
CREATIVE PROCESS	**Encounter** Experience Problem "Challenge"	**Absorption** Engagement/study "Imagining" "Incubation"	**Illumination** Inspiration Revelation "Flash"	**Drafting** Prelim. sketching or "roughing", then "starting"	**Developing** Working out Crafting "Finishing"	**Communication** Display Showing Exhibition	**Response** Criticism Review Evaluation
SCIENTIFIC PROCESS	**Problem** Sensed deficiency "Intelligent bewilderment"	**Observation** Perception: "What goes on?" "Which variables?"	**Illumination** (inductive or inspired)	**Hypothesis** (perhaps selecting one from many)	**Experiment/test** Verification or falsification	**Publication**	**Response** Acceptance or criticism
PROBLEM-SOLVING PROCESS	**Problem** "Felt difficulty" Definition of problem	**Investigation** Perception "Incubation"	**Illumination** Hint of solution	**Formulation** of proposed solution and its possibilities	**Checking** including error elimination and logical verification	**Report** Demonstration Performance	**Response**
WRITING PROCESS	**Experience** Encounter Problem Subject	**Pre-writing** Limit the subject Collect ideas Reflect/discuss	**Inspiration** "See a pattern" "Get a lead" "Get an ending"	**Drafting** Planning or brainstorming; then first draft	**Revision** Self-editing Redrafting Proofreading	**Publication** Showing to another Reading to others Circulation widely	**Response** Appreciation Criticism Evaluation

LEARNING PROCESS

Each of the processes above is a form of "learning process". Terms used for one process may be suitable for others. The titles at the head of the columns may be read as terms which broadly describe "stages" of any disciplined learning process. [Apart from these processes, "learning" includes some other forms: simple reception, imitation, rote/repetition/drill, penalty/reward.] In life, the "stages" of this model are never neatly separated, but flow forward untidily in a "linear" movement which (as the contrary arrows suggest) includes a recursive component as the thinker glances backward to gather data for the next forward move. The whole of each process needs to be seen as potentially creative because meaning can be made at all "stages", not just the "insight" stage.

the best kind of classroom learning must regularly ask: "How can I achieve a depth of understanding [on the next topic] by encouraging at some stage an appropriate piece of writing?" . . .

1. Writing offers itself for use at any or every stage of a learning process, no matter whether this is regarded as a "creative", "scientific", or "problem-solving" process.
2. Writing, through engagement in these thought processes, offers the schools an incidental, comprehensive and cheap how-to-think course; it cultivates careful thinking.
3. Writing can facilitate the deepest possible integration of ideas (and subjects), for it readily draws on, selects and relates ideas from talking, listening, reading, and reflecting.

FINALLY . . .

This article has focused on writing *as a means of learning.* Need I add that writing has many other uses, not least in pleasurable self-expression and literary expression—though both of these too may be broadly viewed as means of learning.

Children learning
through media

CHILDREN LEARNING THROUGH MEDIA

Neville Johnson
Melbourne College of Advanced Education

A variety of experiences contribute to our knowledge. To learn about the culture of another country we may walk in the streets of its cities and towns, ramble through the countryside, talk to the people, eat their foods, examine their arts and crafts and even stay long enough to attempt to live their life-style. On the other hand, if such direct experience is not possible or not sufficient, we may view films and videotapes of aspects of life in that culture, read literature, listen to its music and hear or read commentaries of people who have studied and experienced that culture. In this way we will have substituted or supplemented *direct* experience with *mediated*, or *vicarious*, experience.

One form of experience is not necessarily better than another—each is merely a *different* way of gathering similar information. Thus, both direct and mediated forms of experiencing the culture of a country contribute to the person's conception of that culture, and different experiences are bound to be more appropriate to the purposes and situation of particular people. It will often be the case that direct experience is not an available or convenient option, and, at times, first hand experience might be an unsuitable (or even undesirable) form of learning experience.

Learning through media, or *mediated experience*, is undoubtedly the most prevalent form of experience available to children in their schooling. It is more convenient, economical and acceptable to parents and school administrators. It is also a firmly established convention for the various forms of *language* (e.g. books and "teacher talk") to be the most heavily relied upon mediated experience used in schools. This reliance on media in schools makes it imperative that teachers are aware of both the limitations and the potential of the cultural media.

This article considers the characteristics of both the media and the learner and then examines the nature of the interaction between the child and the medium in a mediated learning experience. From this examination of learning through media a number of implications for teachers are posited.

THE MEDIUM

When considering learning through media it is important for teachers to have a fairly high level of understanding of the forms and characteristics of media.

Each medium is a vehicle, or carrier, of information between a sender and a receiver. The various forms of print media, together with the many forms of visual, audio and audiovisual media, constitute what is often called the cultural media. Each medium shares the characteristic of using a symbol system through which the information is conveyed to the public. Examples of most media forms are to be found in classrooms and schools to be used with, or by, the children.

Some media, such as books, charts, maps, games, pictures and models produce information in a form that is directly available to the child. Other media, such as videotape, audiotape, the various forms of film and the computer disc, require the use of equipment before the information is acceptable to the child. Each medium is available to the child only to the extent that the child is "literate" in that medium.

EDUCATIONAL CHARACTERISTICS OF MEDIA

Although media as a whole, or groups of media, share certain characteristics, each media form has unique characteristics that have educational significance. That is, the media form has characteristics that are of significance to the teacher in teaching and the child in learning. These can be termed the *educational characteristics* of the medium.

Many writers (Gerlach and Ely, 1971; Duane, 1974; Gagne, 1965; Allen, 1967; Kemp, 1971) have generalised about the educational characteristics of media forms. Thus, for example, Duane (1974, p. 34) alerts us to the general characteristics of the book medium which may be of importance to teachers and children. He reminds us that books allow complete random access to both print and visual information and that books allow children to progress at their own rate, selecting their own pace and order of reading, and can thus be classified as having both flexible pacing and flexible sequencing. Similarly, the general educational characteristics of other media forms such as videotape, slides, simulation games and so on, can be listed.

It is interesting to note the contribution of Travers (1970) to our understanding of the general educational characteristics of audio-visual materials. Travers is critical of the notion that multi-media presentations increase learning by virtue of the plurality of media involved. Instead he holds that when too much information is presented through more than one sensory channel simultaneously, or at a very high rate, learning may, in fact, be inhibited.

Listings of the advantages and disadvantages of each medium serve the purpose of alerting the teacher to general educational characteristics of that media form but often fail to focus attention on the characteristics of media that are of most significance to teachers and children wishing to learn through media. To do this, it is preferable to consider a *particular* example of the medium and its *particular* educational characteristics:

- It can hardly be claimed that 16mm films in general are valuable for promoting learning of attitudes, yet the particular film *The Lost Pigeon* (John McDonald, Barr Films) has excellent potential in helping children clarify their values.

- Similarly, it would not be asserted that study prints in general are critical aids to children in their concept learning, but the power of the picture set *The Changing Countryside* (Jorg Muller) to challenge and expand a child's understanding of the concept of "change" is beyond question to teachers and children who have used this particular medium for this purpose.

- The book medium may not be seen to have the general characteristic of stimulating children's minds to fantasy, but *The Phantom Tollbooth* (Norton Juster) does just that for many children.

When considering the educational characteristics of particular examples of a medium a number of factors are important. These include:

1. *The relationship between various aspects of time and the medium*, e.g.:
   - The **audiotape** may be controlled by the child, stopped, rewound and heard again, thus providing variable pacing.
   - The child may be able to take home the **written notes** from the discussion for out-of-class use, thus being provided with more time to make sense of the information.
   - **Photographs** of the excursion or field trip will hold the experience fixed in time, thereby allowing the child to reflect on the substance of the photographs and also to recall events and information that are not captured in the medium, but are remembered because of it.
   - The **telecast** of the event as it happens provides an immediacy that could have a value.

100

- The **time-compressed speech** or **time lapse photography** may allow information to be gathered that would otherwise be unavailable.
2. *The suitability of the medium for a particular group size.* A particular medium may be appropriate for *individuals, small groups* or total *class size* groups, e.g.:
   - A particular **novel** may only be suitable for an individual child to read, whereas *multiple copies* of the novel could allow a group of children to read and discuss it with others.
   - An **overhead transparency** of a map may be an excellent way of indicating particular features to a whole class, whereas the skill-practising activity being undertaken on the **micro-computer** is limited to participation by individuals.
3. *The appropriateness of the particular example of the medium for establishing the learning conditions that facilitate certain types of learning.* This educational characteristic of a medium is demonstrated by a number of examples:
   - An **article** may provide clear and unambiguous information in the form of facts.
   - A set of **study prints** may allow the child to compare and contrast elements in related pictures thus supporting concept formation and the making of generalisations.
   - A **video clip** of a phenomenon in our physical world may

provide an excellent stimulus for hypothesis generation and theory building by children.

- A particular **story** may be powerful in challenging the presently-held attitudes and values of a particular group of children.

4. *The extent to which the particular medium personalises learning.* Two examples may serve to illustrate this characteristic:

    - The *absence* of narration on a **documentary film** could allow children of different ages and with different background knowledge to interact successfully with the medium.
    - **Simulation games** could encourage the child to make decisions, take choices and observe the consequences of these decisions.

5. *The suitability of the medium as a vehicle for communicating, recording or expressing the ideas of the child.* For example:

    - The **model** the child constructs to tell other children what was seen during a direct experience.
    - The **graphs** or **tables** produced to record the information gathered.
    - The **picture story book** that has been made of the topic by the child.
    - The **dance** that is created and performed to share the current level of understanding that a group of children has achieved.

These five characteristics of media are of particular significance to teachers in their curriculum decision-making. Teachers who are aware of the educational characteristics of a particular example of a medium can select appropriate media for their purposes and for the child or children in their class. Children also can be helped to appreciate such characteristics of a medium so that they become more knowledgeable selectors and users of learning materials.

THE CHILD AS A LEARNER

There is a fascinating range of individual differences in school children. There are differences in the extent they are available for learning, the experiences they prefer to learn from, the way and the rate at which they learn, and the sense they make of experiences. These differences lead to the expectation that individual children will respond to mediated learning experiences in different ways.

This expectation is supported by studies of children's thinking which have substantially increased our knowledge of children's learning. It can be asserted that individual children bring to any classroom task an existing knowledge of their world that they use in making sense of the experience and which in turn influences their statements or actions. This knowledge-in-use, or knowledge-in-mind, allows the child to actively process new knowledge into an already well-functioning system. Children may not find the same meaning in a particular experience as adults, but they do actively search after meaning in their own terms. They form *constructs* or hypotheses that work for them at that time. They may, of course, make errors in their construct formation—that is, they form hypotheses about meaning that are incorrect. However, the explanation reached is always plausible to the child, given the knowledge brought to the new experience.

Given this view, the child as a learner shares much with the adult learner. Both children and adults

(a) prefer to be interdependent as well as self directed in their learning;

(b) have a pool of experience to be used to meet immediate learning needs; and

(c) accept the challenge to solve problems that are relevant to them.

Each learner, child or adult, will differ in the knowledge brought to any new learning experience and each will have an individual learning style.

LEARNING THROUGH MEDIA

When a child uses a book, videotape, simulation game or picture, an interaction occurs with that medium. It has been argued earlier that this interaction is best seen as being dynamic, not passive, in nature. That is, individual children bring to the situation their existing and familiar knowledge in an active search for meaning. The knowledge-in-use brought by the child will include two types of knowledge—knowledge of the *content* being considered and knowledge of the *media form.*

Content knowledge includes a range of aspects, including factual information, concepts, principles and generalisations associated with the subject matter; and associated values and attitudes. The child may or may not bring to the mediated experience the appropriate content knowledge. It is possible that the child will have an interest in the subject matter, and some general knowledge of associated facts, but be ignorant of key concepts and principles used in the subject area.

A second type of knowledge is knowledge of the *media form.* The child may or may not bring to a mediated experience sufficient knowledge of the symbol system used in the particular medium to transform an idea into a public image. For example, when using a written language medium, the child requires knowledge of the way written language works (i.e. *syntactic knowledge*). In addition to knowledge of the structure of the symbol system of the medium and the rules for transformation, the child requires sufficient skill in using the medium to attain the intended outcome. That is, the child must be literate in the medium.

MATCH AND MISMATCH SITUATIONS

It follows that when a particular child uses a particular curriculum material, either a situation of *match* or a situation of *mismatch* occurs. Where there is a match between the child and the medium, the child brings sufficient knowledge of both the content and the structure of the medium to allow some sense to be made of the information carried by the medium.

Conversely, a situation of mismatch exists between the child and the medium when the child does not bring sufficient knowledge of the content and the structure of the medium to allow for meaning to be attained.

This view of the nature of the interaction between the child and the medium assumes a *developmental*, rather than a *deficit*, model of learning through media. That is, if a child fails to gain sufficient meaning through the medium it is neither the fault of the child, nor of the medium. There is, rather, a mismatch.

A number of actions are possible in an effort to secure a match between medium and child. The first and most obvious action that could be taken would be to search for another medium. In some cases a *different* book, set of pictures or film is required if the child is to learn. However, the suggestion that this should occur in every case of mismatch has awesome implications for classrooms. Alternative media are not always available and the idea of managing a classroom learning situation where the children are gathering information from completely different curriculum materials is unattractive to most teachers.

The more usual action to be taken in a situation of mismatch between child and medium is to *adapt* the medium and/or *prepare* the child prior for the interaction. Adapting the medium involves intervention by the teacher with knowledge of the intended user in mind. Thus, for example, the written material may be re-written or cut and pasted; a new audiotape prepared for the sound-slide presentation; or a different set of stimulus cards prepared for the simulation game. Preparation of the intended user of the medium could similarly take many forms. The child could be introduced to the special language associated with the topic, or child use of the medium could be delayed until background information has been covered using other learning experiences. Diagrammatically this conception of the relationship between the child and the medium is presented in Figure 1.

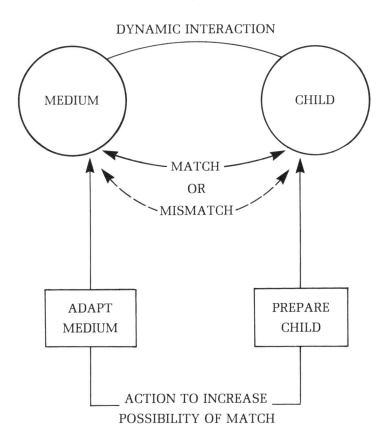

Figure 1: Relationship between Medium and Child.

THE CONCEPT OF "READABILITY" OF THE MEDIUM

It is interesting to note that recent theories of reading (Goodman, 1970; Smith, 1978) claim that "readable" material is that which is *predictable* to the reader. In other words, where there is a match between the material to be read and the reader, the material is readable. However, where a mismatch occurs the material is unable to be read with sufficient understanding. According to the reading literature, a match is more likely to occur when the material

(a) is of interest to the child,

(b) is familiar to the child in that it builds on existing understandings and knowledge about the world,

(c) has language that is meaningful and suitable to the child, in that it allows the child to use existing syntactic knowledge of how language works,

(d) provides a combination of semantic, syntactic and graphophonic cues to make the language predictable to the child,

(e) has an easily identifiable layout and format, with illustrations which provide information and cues, and

(f) has a predictable language style but not a style that is over familiar and boring.

This concept of "readability" has far-reaching consequences for the selection of media. Obviously the use of readability formulae that concentrate solely on the reading material is challenged by this view. The obsession of such formulae with aspects such as vocabulary difficulty and sentence complexity ignores the importance of the particular child's knowledge-in-use as active interaction with the material takes place. The use of "cloze" procedures to select reading materials for use by particular students has a far greater potential.

Similarly, it seems logical that there is a related concept to "readability" for other media forms. Materials that are *viewable* and *listenable* to the child are materials where there is a match between medium and child. For example, a set of slides will be understood by learners at different levels of understanding, with higher understanding resulting when the subject matter of the slides is of interest to the child and builds upon existing understandings and knowledge of the content. In addition, the child viewing the visual representation in the slides needs the appropriate knowledge of how visuals work if a high level of understanding is to be gained.

LEARNING THROUGH THE PRODUCTION OF MEDIA

Earlier in this article the concept of the *educational characteristics* of media was considered. At that time the suitability of the medium as a vehicle for communicating, recording or expressing a child's ideas was considered briefly. This notion of child production of media is important enough to consider here in a little more depth.

It is natural for teachers to first think of media as *something produced by someone else* when considering a child learning through media. The media industry certainly floods the market with commercially prepared media for use in schools. However, media produced by children themselves can make a vital contribution to learning.

As a child gathers information from either a direct or mediated experience, recording of that information often takes place. Numbers of items in particular categories are tallied, interviews are recorded, notes are scribbled, sketches are made and photographs are taken. These actions result in a first order of child production. At this stage the media production is not an articulation of learning but rather a raw record of information gathered.

When the child searches for meaning in these raw data, media may be produced as as integral part of this process. At this second order of child production a bar graph may result from the item tally; the interview notes and sketches may be considered and, as a result, a play written and performed; the photographs may be carefully scrutinised before a model is made or a book written.

In this way, the media produced are vehicles for the articulation of a child's thoughts—expressions of the sense the child has made of the experience. In addition, the creation of the medium may, in itself, alter the meaning that was being expressed. Thus, for example, the act of writing is not merely transmitting the thought of the child, it can also alter the meaning that existed at the time of writing, by allowing a form of review.

If the re-thinking does not occur as a result of the process of media production, it certainly can result from the impact that the product has on others. When a child produces a medium it may communicate information to others and, when this occurs, the meaning expressed is open to discussion and challenge. As a result of this interaction, further learning may occur as the child is urged to re-examine his or her ideas.

Finally, there are additional aspects associated with the act of the production of media by a child which are significant. During the production process a number of things may be

learned by children. They learn:

(a) to choose the medium, the characteristics of which best allow expressions of the particular ideas, images and feelings that they wish to articulate,

(b) that they can use symbols and symbol systems to communicate their thinking to others,

(c) that skills are required in producing media and that these skills refine as they practise them, and

(d) that a sense of satisfaction can result from the production of media.

IMPLICATIONS FOR TEACHERS

Teachers are constantly making arrangements which influence children's learning. Selection of media for use by children is one critical arrangement made as part of a teacher's curriculum decision-making. The view of learning through media that has been discussed in this article has a number of implications for teachers as they work with children. Stated briefly these include:

1. Both *direct* and *mediated experiences* contribute to a child's knowledge of the world: the teacher must choose the form/s of experience which best suit the particular situation and purpose.

2. If mediated experiences are to be used, the teacher should be aware of the *educational characteristics* of the particular medium chosen.

3. When selecting the learning medium, care should be taken to maximise the possibility of a *match* between the particular medium and the child.

4. Whenever possible, *alternative* mediated experiences should be made available to the child so as to increase the challenge and possibility of learning.

5. Teachers should not be obsessed with the use of media to acquire *knowledge.* They should also value the potential of such experiences to further refine *skills in media use* and the associated *intellectual* skills.

6. *Teacher skill* in media use and production is a significant factor in ensuring effective use and production of media by children. Where teachers can demonstrate careful selection and creative production and use of media, they provide useful models for children.

7. Production of media by children should be encouraged by teachers as a means of recording, expressing and communicating ideas, images and feelings. The notion that written language is the only legitimate form of recorded communication should be avoided and production of visual and other media forms encouraged, especially in young children.

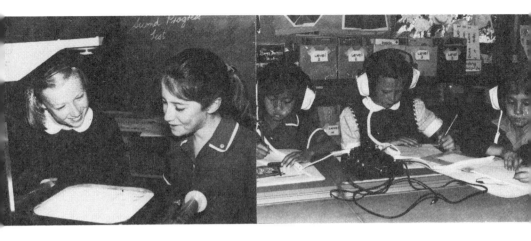

REFERENCES

Allen, W.H., "Media Stimulus and Types of Learning" in *Audiovisual Instruction*, Jan., 1967, pp. 27-31.

Dodge, M. *et al.*, "How Teachers Perceive Media" in *Educational Technology*, Jan., 1974, pp. 21-24.

Duane, J.E., "Media as Applied to Individualised Instruction" in *Audiovisual Instruction*, May, 1974, pp. 33-36.

Eisner, E.W., "The Contribution of Painting to Children's Cognitive Development" in *Journal of Curriculum Studies*, Vol. 11, No. 2, 1979, pp. 109-116.

Gagne, R.M., *The Conditions of Learning*, New York, Holt Rinehart and Winston, 1965.

Gerlach, V.S. and Ely, D., *Teaching and Media*, Englewood Cliffs (New Jersey), Prentice Hall, 1971.

Goodman, K., "Reading; a psycholinguistic guessing game", in Ruddel and Singer, *Theoretical Models and Processes in Reading*, International Reading Association, 1970.

Johnson, N., "Resources for Curricula and Learning; issues and strategies". Papers presented at the Third Workshop *Coordinating the School's Learning Resources*, Burnie (Tas.), November 9-10, 1976.

Johnson, N., "Resource Networks and the Curriculum" in *Curriculum and Research Bulletin*. Publications Branch, Education Department of Victoria, Vol. xi, No. 3, August, 1976, pp. 82-89.

Johnson, N., "The Role of the Teacher-Librarian in Curriculum Decision-making" in *Society for Mass Media and Resources Technology*, Vol. 10, No. 3, 1980, pp. 27-43.

Kelly, G.A., "A Brief Introduction to Personal Construct Theory" in D. Bannister (ed.), *Perspectives in Personal Construct Theory*, London, Academic Press, 1966.

Kemp, J.E., "Which Medium?" in *Audiovisual Instruction*, Dec., 1971, pp. 32-36.

Olsen, D.R. and Bruner, J.S., "Learning Through Experience and Learning Through Media" in D.R. Olsen (ed.), *Media and Symbols; the forms of expression, communication and education*, 73rd Year Book, N.S.S.E., 1975, Ch. 6.

Sinha, C. and Walkerdine, V., "Children, Logic and Learning" in M. Horles (ed.), *Changing Childhood*, Writers and Readers Publishing Cooperative, 1979.

Smith, F., *Reading*, London, Cambridge University Press, 1978.

Smith, F., *Writing and the Writer*, London, Heinemann Educational Books, 1982.

Taylor, K., "Media in the Context of Instruction" in *School Media Quarterly*, Vol. 4, No. 3, Spring 1976, pp. 224-8, 237-41.

Travers, R.M.W., *Man's Information System*, Scranton (Pa.), Chandler, 1970.

LEARNING THROUGH DATA BASES

Tony Moore
Casula High School (N.S.W.)

Wayne Roberts
Belmore North Public School (N.S.W.)

It is all too easy to view a computer as a personal video game arcade or, worse still, as an electronic blackboard. If computers are to play a valuable and not a destructive role in the learning process, then schools must come to terms with what it is that computers do best that cannot already be done effectively in the classroom. Motivation alone is not sufficient justification. Even more importantly, teachers have to consider the thinking and learning done by children using computers. The child using a computer as a video game may develop manual dexterity and physical co-ordination; the child being subjected to the electronic blackboard may well be able to bark (or type) instant responses to appropriate stimuli. But after twenty years of trying to extinguish such behaviour from humanities classrooms do we really want to resurrect these old responses in a glossier form? We know they work and we know that computers make them work even better. We also know a lot about the effect of those teaching/learning practices on children's thinking processes, and on their ability to think independently and make sense of their world.

So what else do computers do well? Their basic function is the storage of information which can be quickly and easily retrieved (or accessed) according to the user's requirements. Such information and retrieval functions are contained in programs known as *data bases*. In the classroom (or library) they can perform the role of electronic encyclopaedias with automatic entry through electronic indexes.

In the child's thinking this use develops an awareness of what a computer can do in the context of the real world of information—a practical application of classification and indexing skills—and it develops the skill of questioning. These are of real importance in their own right. Furthermore, children can use the facts contained in relevant data bases for their own work. They research a data base in the same way they would research a book and learn from it that which is relevant to their needs.

A major move in the teaching of humanities from the seventies into the eighties has been an awareness of the value of *original writing* in the learning process. In the sixties we would often accept, indeed praise, the pretty project with slabs of copied notes which were, at least, relevant. We had the conviction that learning by reading was taking a key role in the child's acquisition of knowledge and projects were clear evidence of some reading. We have to come to learn, through the work of Britton, Moffett, Graves, Murray, Walshe and others, some of the relationships that exist between composing and learning. Children are doing fewer projects and, instead, are creating real *books* for real purposes—they are read by real readers. Through producing books of their own, children are learning not only writing skills and processes, but greater knowledge of content, of information and its flexibility. Pupil-created books are becoming important instruments in cognitive growth.

This awareness is being carried over into the area of computers and data bases. There are a number of commercial programs, e.g. *PFS* (Personal Filing System), *List Handler* and others which enable the users to create their own data bases. Teachers are beginning to use these programs to enable children to create their own data bases. The creation of such

data bases requires of the user the following activities and skills:

(i) to set the limits of the topic or data area;

(ii) to acquire the relevant data;

(iii) to set up classification and grouping criteria;

(iv) to classify data according to the criteria;

(v) to set out and formulate the criteria into a workable, accessible system;

(vi) to enter the data;

(vii) to test the classification system and, if necessary, modify it according to its accessibility or usefulness.

These are the minimum activities required if the product is to function as an effective data base. This is what children are now creating—effective data bases for other children to use, expand or modify. *Publication and response are just as important here as in creative writing.*

What are the children deriving from this creative process? They are researching, gathering, accepting, rejecting, modifying and classifying information. They are translating abstract concepts into concrete form. They are engaging in an hypothesising/testing process and the test occurs in real conditions for real purposes.

Data bases lend themselves to topic areas that are relevant and real to pupils. There is richness in the language of explanation between pupils at various levels in coming to terms with the concepts they are trying to express. It is a wonderful teaching experience to watch three or four pupils engaged in heated debate about how a controversial item should be classified. Topics can be as simple or as complex as the interests or levels demand. Certainly infants children have created data bases about their family or their class friends. Their classification is in terms with which they can cope, e.g. according to age, sex, relationship to one person, physical features etc. The range of possibilities covers the whole of primary or secondary education in all subject areas.

If we accept that *writing* as a composing process is valuable for learning, then let us be open to the use of *computers* as a potential tool in this learning process. Word processing is an obvious use and the creation of data bases can be extremely effective. These are uses of the computer which are more than consistent with enlightened humanities curricula.

Footnote

If you come to accept the premises of this article then look to Seymour Papert's computer language program *Logo* as an extension of the use of the computer to aid critical and cognitive growth.

CAN CHILDREN LEARN FROM TELEVISION— AND IF SO—WHAT?

Frank Meaney
Community Relations and Information Unit
N.S.W. Department of Education

Television and History have had to endure a common slander levelled against them, usually couched in the form, "History (or Television) teaches that . . ." and then followed by some statement calculated to raise emotion and ire in the listener. History or Television cannot, of themselves, be said to have ever *taught* anybody anything. However, many thousands of people have *learned* a great deal from a study of History and many hundreds of thousands have *learned*, and will continue to do so, from the modern technological marvel of Television.

The point at issue is really whether television "teaches" by stealth, in a sense impinging upon the consciousness of humans without their knowing and thus in some strange way causing people to learn things that, if they had their druthers, they would prefer not to know.

This fear of the new or unknown is common to humans everywhere and is a classic first generation response. Soon it is followed by a plan of action to enable humans, especially children, to combat the influence of the new and so develop an immunity of a kind—the so-called *innoculation* system of education.

It is time perhaps to move away from that kind of response towards a positive, soundly-based appreciation of some of the roles television can play in the lives of children—and does play for the greatest number of Australian children. *One of the obvious requirements for any learning program is that there is regular, frequent contact between the learner and the information source, whether it be mechanical or human.*

Television is a sought-after medium of dispensing information in Australian homes, according to available survey data. In Sydney, Melbourne, Brisbane and Adelaide 99% of all homes have television sets and at least 95% of these homes have colour television whilst at least 33% of homes have more than one television set.[1] Quite obviously the child learner has his/her tools to hand.

Having established the *availability* of the tools, it is instructive to determine whether the tools are in regular *use*. Some previous surveys of the viewing habits of children have revealed some remarkable *tours de force*, one classic case being of a young teenage girl watching TV for 105 hours per week.

Dr. Patricia Edgar claims that the average viewing time by children of television is about 23 hours per week, with about 20% of children viewing for more than 40 hours per week.[2] An interesting sidelight to this voluntary association with the information source (television) is that most *parents* seem to have little idea of the amount of time spent by their own children watching television. The Australian Broadcasting Tribunal conducted a survey in Sydney, Melbourne, Brisbane and Adelaide in 1977/78 and found that parents of 10-12 year old children *underestimated* the amount of time their children watched television. Of the children questioned 55% said they watched television whilst doing their homework whilst about 54% of parents reported that their children *never* watched television whilst doing homework.

WHAT DO CHILDREN WATCH?

One of the illuminating factors to emerge from a study of children's television viewing is to examine what primary school children watch. One wrong assumption is that children generally watch children's programs and adolescents and adults watch programs made for older audiences. In Australia, Monday to Friday, there are broadcast between 4 and 5 p.m. programs which are made specifically for children aged 6-13, i.e. primary school children. However, whilst it is recognised that children do have many other things to do between 4 and 5 p.m., it is curious that, in Sydney, about 15.6% of the total 5-12 year old audience watched "children's" programs whilst 22.8% watched *A Country Practice* and 22.4% of this same age group watched *Perfect Match*—both programs designed, one would have thought, for a much older audience.

This survey data reveals what was mostly known, i.e. that the whole gamut of television programming is wide open to primary school children, regulated only by parental and other adult control. The technology is embarrassingly simple and it is

114

quite obviously being taken advantage of. Consequently, it does not make very much educational sense to examine the question as to *what* children learn from television by trying to examine the *content* of particular programs and deciding whether the learning has been "good" or "bad", acceptable or unacceptable. Educators have to accept that the learning which will occur by children watching television is thoroughly individualistic and will depend to a very great deal on the child itself.

THE NATURE OF TELEVISION

It is possible to make some statements about the content of television programs and argue that, from watching a depiction of X, it is possible for a child to learn Y. However, this is a thoroughly exhausting process for any teacher and has little point because of the vagaries of personal experience. It is more useful to proceed *from the nature of television itself* and make some general statements from which a teaching program can be developed which would be applicable to all students.

Television is a "window on the world" for almost all the children who watch it. The fact that, through the medium of television, it is possible for very great numbers of children to be exposed to information about a whole range of issues, places, people and things means that *the possibility exists that learning something about those elements will occur.* The type of learning will vary from child to child, depending upon background, intellect, values and skills. But it is almost impossible to contemplate situations where no learning will occur. Even the most poorly equipped viewer will learn. If there is skilled intervention of a third-party, the chances of learning opportunities occurring are greatly enhanced. A great deal depends on the *quality* of that intervention.

TELEVISION AND REALITY

Another general statement about television and learning which is worth consideration is that *television, of itself, acts upon, changes or modifies the information it transmits.* The content of television is thought of by viewers as being "real" because of its close relationship to life. Thus, it is often assumed that the output *is* reality. Nothing is further from the truth. Television produces, for consumption, *representations* of reality. This was no more apparent than in the televised opening of the 1984 Olympic Games when viewers were treated to a direct telecast of the official opening. This television event had much more built into it than what would have been experienced by an actual spectator or participant in the Los Angeles Coliseum. Television *built upon* that experience, with producers deciding which of many points of view or camera locations would follow one another to create a very different reality from the "warm", limited experience of any person who might have been present. The factors which were at work in fashioning the teleview of that event are unknown to most people but, to an estimated audience of 2.5 billion, the "reality" they experienced was the work of a very few.

LEARNING TO "READ" TELEVISION

If it is possible to accept the above then it is apparent that if children are to learn from television some clear ideas have to emerge as to what can be learned. Dr Len Masterman of Nottingham University has been one of the workers in this field who has had some impact on Australian thinking. In an important paper delivered to the National Media Education Conference in Adelaide in 1982 Masterman argued that children need to be taught (and therefore be given the opportunity to learn) about four central issues:

1. Who are responsible for the "realities" constructed by television?
2. How are these constructed "realities" made to appear as natural and real?
3. What are the characteristics of the televised "reality"?
4. How does the audience "read" or "decode" the "reality" created by television?

Primary school children will not, by their nature, be able to deal with these central ideas in the same depth and to the same degree as older students, but it is important that these questions underlie any program of teaching children about television. Not all questions would be dealt with at the same time or necessarily in the order outlined above but at a time appropriate to the group.

If it is regarded as important for primary school children to know who are responsible for the "realities" constructed by television then it becomes a relatively simple task to devise learning situations where this will occur. Drawing upon other disciplines, skills can be developed which will allow children to discover the various tasks which have to be carried out before a particular program comes to air. If, for example, the topic of "News" is approached, it is almost universally possible, through analysis of news items, to discover the methods used to transform a mere occurrence to the status of a news item. This is not the place for detailed analysis of a teaching situation but, if a news item (say, local news) is tracked from occurrence until it is telecast, it becomes abundantly clear how many people are involved in the task. Realisation of the nature of news construction can then be utilised to determine the agents who construct other programs and the proper relationship between actors,

116

directors, producers and those who contribute the money to make it all possible.

It should now be patently obvious that if skilled persons are able to construct programs which are so "realistic" as to be thought of as being "real" then it will be necessary to spend time learning how to pierce this apparent reality as a matter of self-defence. By helping children recognise what is going on we may prevent them from having the wool pulled over their eyes.

The skills necessary are not new and are at use already in other parts of the school curriculum. In the field of Art, for example, children have been learning, for a long time, the effect of various techniques on views of reality. Practical work involving even simple photographs from the family album is a good place to start. The effects created by cropping, adding and positioning in relation to other photographs is soon appreciated by children.

It is not difficult in today's classrooms to move towards some "hands-on" experience so that children learn, by doing, some of the skills of program construction. This process is significant in allowing children to appreciate the nature of the skills involved rather than worrying about the quality of the finished product.

With a growing realisation of the nature of the skills of visual literacy, children can be introduced to the complementary nature of sound. This can be done merely by utilising the sound level control on a television set. A product on television without sound becomes a very different product, capable of many different interpretations.

"Hands-on" experience is a very significant element in allowing children to realise the role the selection of images plays in constructing media products. Photographs or slides can illustrate the principle very well and it is possible to explore the variety of effects which can be gained by ordering and re-ordering a series of pictures or slides. Out of activities such as these grows an understanding of one of the central principles relating to television, i.e. that every item telecast is the product of somebody's decisions. No matter how "real" that item does appear it is a *particular* "reality", rather than the *only* reality.

Quite obviously, too, it is appropriate to introduce to children the notion of the effect the *frame* has upon our perception of reality. Selection is aided by the framing of the television camera and, although the action portrayed may appear to be the "total reality", it is only a part—that part within the framing device or camera. There are many ways this can be demonstrated, using experiences from other subjects such as Art and Science.

The Brady Bunch—whose version of "reality"?

When the question of the common characteristics of televised reality is raised one of the key issues emerges. Why does television deal with some issues and not with others? Why are some things-always "on" television? What happened to the headline issues of yesterday? And the day before? The answer lies in an understanding of what is called *agenda setting*. That is, television makers decide what the *agenda* will be in homes and then, having selected the issues, they decide how these issues will be dealt with and how they should be interpreted. Even at primary school level it is possible for students to develop an understanding of the relationship between television and such things as fires, gory accidents and engineered clashes with the police. It is not a long step from there to a discussion about why these events are presented in the ways they are, i.e. the "angle" that is taken. Discussion can soon uncover other possible angles—and lead to questions about why they are not used as often as the dominant angle.

Value education is a concept which has been around for a long time and has an honourable relationship with television. Through television it is possible to present a *range* of ideas or, perhaps, a *few* ideas in a range of forms so as to ensure that other, opposing, ideas are kept out of the picture. It is patently obvious that school systems in this country have taught children a range of values over a great period of time—even if Civics and Citizenship as subject areas may not appear in official curricula. Television, through the "reality" it decides to present, reproduces, over and over again, ideas and values which often are taken for granted. One example which is often used to demonstrate this process is the program *The Brady Bunch*. There was a long period during which acceptance of the values exhibited in that program was high but, when women began to become vocal about their roles, they repudiated the artificial "ideal life" presented in that program. It would not be difficult to show how the values in that program reflected dominant ideas of the time in the society in which the program was created.

Once that link is demonstrated it is possible to use the techniques of analysis common in every classroom to draw conclusions about the ideas presented in popular television programs and the dominant ideas in the culture. If that concept is pursued, a giant step will have been taken towards the development of a critical, thinking person.

When one begins to consider how audiences react to programs on television, the issue is usually clouded by *ratings*, regarded by the financiers of television as the measure of success of programs. The ratings are a gross measure at best, indicating the size of the share of the available audience a par-

119

ticular program has. Individuals, however, react individually but some research findings in the Eisenhower report of the early sixties indicated that the degree of learning from television programs bore a close relationship, inversely, to the degree of learning from other, more conventional sources. If a child lived in a supportive relationship with relatives (such as parents), enjoyed a formal schooling program and had strong church affiliation, then dependence on television, by that child, for social learning was low. On the other hand, if children obtained little social learning from the traditional sources, there was greater dependence on television. What this all means is that the traditional teachers of children have strong competition and, for many children, television is an attractive, compelling medium dispensing information in a wide range of areas but none of it unbiased or uninfluenced by others.

Television learning is influenced, in the first instance, by parents and other out-of-school factors. Teachers can make a decided impact too. However, it is a fact that many teachers disqualify themselves as potential *partners* in a child's whole learning process because of a difficulty they have in *sharing* a child's knowledge base, especially that base which comes from television.

The gap which existed for a considerable time between adult viewing and child viewing is closing, with children watching many of the same programs as adults. Whether teachers watch the same programs as do children is not really known but sample those programs they must, as only then can realistic dialogue be set up between the two.

The relationship between teacher and child is still one of the most significant in the learning process. It has passed through many stages since the advent of television: hostility because television was more attractive than schoolwork; amazement at the ability of children to endure cold, hunger and exhaustion to watch television; as a scapegoat because children fell asleep at school (poor parenting was a more reasonable explanation); disdain at the emergence of popular culture; accommodation with the realisation that television is here to stay.

Some kind of Mass Media Education based on the principles mentioned above will, it is hoped, distinguish the next phase.

REFERENCES
1. *N.B.* All data in this article is taken from analyses of *NcNair Anderson* television survey data prepared by Australian Broadcasting Tribunal staff, Quarter 1, 1984.
2. Edgar, P., *Children and Television Policy Implications*. Melbourne, Australian Children's Television Foundation, 1983.